The Historic Hotels of Ireland

A Select Guide

WENDY ARNOLD

The Historic Hotels of Ireland

A Select Guide

Photographs by
ROBIN MORRISON

THAMES AND HUDSON

For Joyce Bragdon Arnold

Map: Hanni Bailey

Typeset in Monophoto Plantin Light

Printed and bound in Spain
D.L.TO: 26-1989

Contents

Preface

The romantic silhouette of Ashford Castle rises above its immaculate golf course. See page 17.

Irish hotels have a habit of living up to their promises. Battlemented castles stand by the shores of salmon-rich rivers; fine Georgian mansions look out over rolling parkland; white painted, gray-roofed cottages perch on the sweeping mountain slopes of Connemara, where wild-maned white ponies roam; snug, slate-hung houses are tucked into sheltering ports crammed with gaily-painted fishing boats. Waterford crystal chandeliers glitter, flower-filled gardens are tended with loving care, and at several hotels the local hunt meets before the front door. Gourmet travelers will rejoice in the fresh seafood, wild game, and home-grown produce, find wine-lists well-supplied with good vintages, and should not leave Ireland without sampling Irish whiskey and velvet-smooth draught Guinness – quite unlike the fizzy bottled variety.

It is, however, the warmth of the welcome which sets Ireland apart from all other countries I have visited. Too often elsewhere hotelkeeping has become a polished business enterprise, in which the owners' interest in a larger bank-balance seems to outweigh their interest in a happier guest. By contrast, Ireland offers a friendly greeting that is never obsequious. On my travels I encountered porters who shook me warmly by the hand, introduced themselves by name, and asked with real interest about my journey; the chambermaid who turned down my bed in one hotel told me that she thought the Queen of England "is a fine woman;" and in one dining room, the waiter, having discussed the menu with interest, added, "sure, the food here is grand." There are luxurious hotels with vast bedrooms, impressive marble bathrooms, large colour TVs, rapid room service, and highly skilled chefs, yet still their staff remain warmly interested in people.

In the course of my research, I drove several thousand miles by myself round the Republic of Ireland, exploring remote corners, back-tracking to find hotels tucked away beside inland loughs or hidden bays, and houses invisible on vast private estates. As with my previous books, on the historic hotels of Scotland, France, London, and the English countryside, the hotels which I eventually chose to include have not paid to be in this book, neither have I accepted any special treatment from them. The final selection was made only after much heart-searching: some owners were so deliciously eccentric and their hotels so magnificently decrepit that I yearned to include them, but on balance judged that they would be enjoyed only by those with a strong spirit of adventure. Friendliness was not enough: the hotels I have included all offer comfort as well as historic charm. I did not include even architecturally magnificent establishments with titled owners if I thought they were not whole-heartedly committed to cherishing guests, or if facilities were *too* basic.

The dividing line between a family-run hotel and a private house receiving paying guests is somewhat blurred. I have included several private houses, for I find that when families are enthusiastic about offering hospitality, they can provide a very special welcome. In Ireland I discovered some irresistible mansions, in varying states of picturesque antiquity, all with delightful owners. Splendid rooms were furnished with much-loved heirlooms and family portraits – even family ghosts. Your hostess will often double as cook, producing freshly baked cakes for tea and an excellent dinner. Your host may take you shooting or fishing, accompanied by an expert ghillie. You will be received as a family friend and will soon find yourself drawn into the life of the local village.

Do not demand international standards of perfection everywhere in Ireland, but I would be surprised if its charm did not captivate you, as it captivated me. Here are thirty hotels and private homes that I can without hesitation recommend to everybody looking for Irish hospitality at its most memorable.

General Information

Preparation Few hotels in Ireland are custom-built, so it is important to decide before booking exactly what your priorities are, and to ask for a room accordingly. Is the view more important than a shower over the bathtub? Will you have to climb several flights of stairs, or is there an elevator? Do you mind if the castle which is full of priceless family antiques also has bathtubs which are timeworn period pieces, or would you rather select the refurbished mansion with the modern plumbing? Can you live without TV and a telephone in your room? Remember to check on details – the actual width of the romantic four-poster, for instance (it may be only 4 ft 6 in), the size of the room, and closet capacity. Read entries carefully, then check with owners by phone, to avoid disappointment. Travel agents may get you better rates at the larger hotels.

Do not forget to bring light raincoats, even in summer. Ireland is so green because it rains frequently, but seldom for long at a time. Should the weather turn cold, reasonably priced, excellent woollens are widely available. If you wish to make use of any hotel's sporting facilities – shooting, fishing, etc. – notify the hotel when booking.

Terms Since prices can alter rapidly, I have divided the hotels into three broad categories, based on the complete cost for dinner (without wine) for *two* people, and a standard double room with continental breakfast for one night. I have included taxes and service (though these are sometimes charged separately). When booking ask what is included in the price, and book your dinner table. I have not included the cost of *à la carte* meals, drinks, or telephone calls. Enquire about special breaks, off-season bargains, and all-inclusive sporting holidays. NB Not all places accept credit cards, but most accept dollar or sterling checks. (Note that Mastercard is the British Access card.) Verify the method of payment when booking. Prices are all in Irish pounds (IR£ or *punts*) which can be confusing if you are used to thinking in pounds sterling. The approximate equivalents are based on a rate of IR£1.00 = $1.46 or £0.84 sterling.

Moderate   IR£50–100 ($ 73–146/£ 42– 84)
Expensive   IR£101–150 ($148–219/£ 85–126)
Deluxe   IR£175–270 ($256–394/£147–226)

When staying in a private house where no service is charged, ask the hostess whether it is customary to leave a tip for the ghillie or daily help.

Getting there and sightseeing International flights come in only to Shannon; one can also fly from England to Dublin, Cork, and Knock (nr Galway).

Rental cars are expensive, but beware choosing the smallest size if planning long trips on poor-surface back-roads. From Britain, car-ferries can make the crossing in as little as $3\frac{1}{2}$ hours. If entering the Republic from Northern Ireland, note that the border may be crossed only at authorized points.

It is essential to have a detailed road map or atlas (Ordnance Survey are good) if touring. A car compass also helps – the national sport of village youths is turning signposts to point in the wrong direction. Note that modern road signs are in kilometers, but old ones are in miles, which can be confusing. When planning an itinerary, allow generous time between destinations. Distances appear short, but even main "N" roads can be narrow and winding, though they are being improved (causing delays at roadworks). Main roads out of Dublin are mostly good; in the countryside many roads have only one lane on each side, with a wide hard shoulder onto which people often draw to allow you to pass. It usually takes about four hours to cross the country from side to side on the N roads; on side roads allow for maximum 30 miles per hour average. Drive cautiously round corners: you may meet, as I did, unexpected flocks of sheep or cows, farmers moving a large untethered bull to the next field, tractors drawing laden hay-carts, mothers walking babies in strollers, horse-drawn painted gypsy caravans, a street cattle market without pens, crowds coming out of church, or rival teams of men playing the local game of bowling a large metal ball along a measured mile (fewest throws wins). I have suggested routes to each hotel from Dublin, but it is always worth asking hotels how best to reach them. Most hotels can arrange for a local taxi or limousine and chauffeur to drive anyone discouraged by the above.

Private houses John Colclough has organized an association of private houses offering accommodation: Hidden Ireland, P.O. Box 2281, Dublin 4, tel: (01) 686463; he also personally conducts tours. In the English Manner, Lancych, Boncath, Pembrokeshire, Wales SA37 0LJ, tel: (0239) 77378 or (0285) 75267, or Elegant Ireland, 15 Harcourt St, Dublin 2, tel: (01) 751665 or 751632, will also organize bookings, mainly in stately homes.

A footnote I am confident that the owners and managers of the hotels and houses I have chosen will be friendly and helpful. If a problem should arise, please point it out to them personally, as they will be glad to be informed; tell them also of anything that specially pleased you. I too am grateful for comments; please write to me care of the publishers.

An alphabetical index of hotels and their locations appears on page 96.

N

NORTHERN

IRELAND

REPUBLIC

OF

IRELAND

Donegal

Belfast

Sligo

Ballina

Knock

Westport

Clifden

Galway

Gort

Shannon Airport

Limerick

Kilkenny

Cashel

Waterford

Wexford

Dublin

Wicklow

Killarney

Cork

Bantry

① ②③④⑤⑥⑦⑧⑨⑩⑪⑫⑬⑭⑮⑯⑰⑱⑲⑳㉑㉒㉓㉔㉕㉖㉗㉘㉙㉚

0   60 Mls

0   100 Km

Castlehill
Co. Mayo

Georgian inheritance

The last great mansion remaining in the north of Mayo, Enniscoe House has been named a Heritage House of Ireland, and is one of the treasures of the Irish Georgian Society. It is owned by Susan Kellett, a cousin of the Earl of Mount Charles; her brother, a fine-art consultant, manages the estate's rare woodcock shoot. Her mother's family, the Bourkes, once owned these lands, but were dispossessed by Cromwell. By Susan's parents' marriage, the original owners and the family who held the estate from 1660 were united.

The oldest part of the house, three-storeyed and known to date at least from 1740, has massively thick walls which suggest a yet earlier fortified farmhouse. In the 1790s the owner of the house had become prosperous and built for his wife a more imposing Georgian exterior to enclose the original building, adding on a lofty new front hall, an elegant pair of high-ceilinged reception rooms, and a staircase twirling gently up to an oval landing lit by a delicately ornamented dome.

The hall is filled with family portraits, mementos and crests, an enormous 37lb mounted pike, and a pair of early fishing rods. The drawing room is formal, with gracious antiques; the sitting room has plump inviting armchairs. The low-ceilinged dining room, where Susan Kellett provides excellent homecooking, is in the original part of the house. The three bedrooms at the front of the house are enormous and high-ceilinged. Of their bathrooms, one is modern and ensuite, another vast and across the hall, the third original, mahogany, and reached through a dressing room. The small, friendly bedrooms at the back are at the top of a sturdy ancient staircase.

The house has two ghosts, one said to be seen in the overgrown pleasure-grounds where he was buried after a riding accident, and the other the butler whose gentle presence lingers in the old basement kitchen. Today's kitchen is on the ground floor, in the former estate office, with all the compartments for receiving rent still preserved.

Enniscoe House stands in 150 acres, and owns two islands in the lake (a ghillie – who is a great personality – is on hand to help fishermen). Sometimes the house is let entirely to a family group, with the owner popping in to cook meals if required. To own such a treasure is a joy, a despair, a pride, and an endless battle against the surprises that historic houses can spring. Repair of the plasterwork in the dome over the stairs and restoration of the pleasure-grounds overwhelmed by the woodland must await the coming of some benevolent benefactor. Nonetheless, this is a house of great individuality whose delightful owner makes all her guests extremely welcome.

Family heirlooms furnish this dignified house (above): opposite is the sitting room (above) and one of the bedrooms; overleaf is the formal drawing room.

ENNISCOE HOUSE, Castlehill, nr Crossmolina, Ballina, Co. Mayo. **Tel.** Ballina (096) 31112. **Telex** c/o 40855. **Fax** No. **Owner** Mrs Susan Kellett. **Open** 1 April–1 Oct. **Rooms** 7 double, 4 with own bathroom (1 with hand shower, 2 with wall shower). **Facilities** Drawing room, sitting room, dining room, gardens, lake with 2 islands, 150-acre grounds. Fishing (boat and ghillie), woodcock shoot, riding nearby by arrangement. Helicopter landing. **Lunch** No. **Restrictions** None. **Terms** Expensive (includes full breakfast). **Credit cards** Access, Amex, Visa. **Getting there** N4 to Longford, N5 to Swinford, N57 to Crossmolina (165 miles, 4 hrs). 131 miles from Shannon. **Nearest airport** Knock. **Nearest rail station** Ballina. **Of local interest** Archaeological sites; lake drives. **Whole day expeditions** Sligo; Achill Island; Westport House; Connemara. **Refreshments** Pubs and small restaurants in Ballina and Westport (ask owner). **Dining out** Newport House, Newport (see p. 15).

2 Newport House

A fisherman's riverside retreat

Kieran Thompson, a geophysicist who has traveled the world, was glad to return with his wife, Thelma, to his native Ireland, to begin a new life as a hotelier. In 1985 they took over Newport House from the widow of Francis Mumford-Smith, whose father, a renowned fisherman, had so loved his fishing holidays in this area that he had come to live here in 1945. The house, with private fisheries on the tidal Newport river, was established by the Mumford-Smiths as a fishing hotel and the Thompsons have continued this tradition, retaining many of the long-serving staff. Newport House is now a member of the Relais et Châteaux Association.

The house itself is very interesting. Built on a far older site, up on the river bank, a pretty 1720s bow-fronted mansion has been encased in a later extremely grand edifice. The sitting room, with chandelier and fine fireplace, has doors at one end which are curiously asymmetrical, since they were cut through into an enormous dining room added later to the end of the building. Huge windows throw light on vast oil-paintings, and the broad pale gold stripes of the wallpaper. An enormous drawing room directly above is being refurbished. Behind the modest original hall opens an unexpectedly vast inner hall, proudly graced by the famous monster Mumford-Smith prize pike. A staircase rises up to a galleried landing, topped by a splendid plasterwork ceiling with a heat-gobbling glass skylight. My high-ceilinged bedroom retained its original wooden shutters. The bed was comfortable and the bathroom large. Other grander bedrooms have massive four-posters, and look out over gardens sloping down towards the river.

Dinner in the imposing dining room was good: the Thompsons' smoked salmon, a tasty chicken broth, a delicate gourmet version of traditional Irish stew, with perfectly-cooked vegetables and a bowl of salad as well, some local cheese in prime condition, and a tangy rhubarb tart. The Thompsons themselves eat each night in the restaurant, which helps them to keep in touch with their guests' reactions. After dinner coffee is served in the sitting room, or on the other side of the hall in a small room which leads out of the friendly bar, where local people and guests mingle. When Newport House is full, fishermen wishing to dine at the hotel are sometimes recommended to stay in the small convent next door, where kind nuns provide very simple, spotlessly clean rooms for travelers. But you do not need to be a fisherman to enjoy your stay at Newport House.

The lofty stairwell (opposite) has impressive plasterwork; above is the creeper-clad entrance front.

NEWPORT HOUSE, Newport, Co. Mayo. **Tel.** Newport (098) 41222. **Telex** 53740. **Fax** No. **Owners** Kieran and Thelma Thompson. **Manager** Owen Mullins. **Open** 20 March–1 Oct. **Rooms** 17 double, 2 single, all with bathroom and direct-dial phone. **Facilities** Drawing room, 2 sitting rooms, bar, dining room, billiards, garden and grounds. Fishing in lake and sea. Riding, golf, tennis and squash available locally, by arrangement. Helicopter landing. **Lunch** Yes. **Restrictions** No pets in main house. **Terms** Expensive (includes full breakfast). **Credit cards** All major cards. **Getting there** N6, N4, N5 to Castlebar, R311 to Newport (164 miles, 4 hrs). 100 miles from Shannon. **Nearest airport** Knock. **Nearest rail station** Westport. **Of local interest** Burrishoole Abbey (ruin); Westport House; coastal road drives; Connemara. **Whole day expeditions** Achill Island; Connemara. **Refreshments** Pubs and restaurants in Westport (ask owner). **Dining out** Ashford Castle, Cong (see p. 17); Enniscoe House, Castlehill (by arrangement only, see p. 11).

Battlemented luxury

Ashford Castle stands at the head of Lough Corrib. You drive in under an impressive gateway, through a manicured nine-hole golf-course, and across an arched bridge over a wide river, into a broad forecourt, where the massive partly 13th-century crenelated castle stretches before you. In the 1800s the castle was rebuilt as a hunting lodge, and it was further extended while in the ownership of the Guinness family. In 1971 it became a hotel, mainly for fishermen, but has since been totally refurbished, and is now a splendid 83-bedroom luxury establishment, under American ownership.

Although a moat of river and lake and a curtain wall with battlements and watchtowers still remain, the castle's courtyard is now filled by immaculate flower gardens tended by fourteen gardeners. The jaunting car used by John Wayne and Maureen O'Hara in *The Quiet Man*, filmed on location here in 1952, is owned by the castle. Complete with a glossy pony and a well-turned-out groom, it can be hired by guests for outings in the grounds. Tied up by the hotel is a magnificent launch which once belonged to the liner *Queen Elizabeth II*, on which guests may cruise the lake. A well-polished Landrover with a tweed-suited ghillie is also on hand if you wish to go shooting.

After entering the castle, guests first encounter two suits of armour, before turning right into a large panelled hall to be greeted by the efficient and friendly desk staff. A large hospitality desk is spread with all the touring, sight-seeing, and sporting information you could possibly want, and there are glass cases of mounted prize fish, and glorious arrangements of fresh flowers. A second hallway has a flight of steps leading straight up to the next floor, and a finely-carved balcony. A gourmet dining room on the right – reached through an anteroom containing an enormous ornate fireplace large enough to sit in –

is hung in peacock-blue silk, with gilt-framed mirrors and a view over gardens, lake, and hills beyond. The main dining room is huge, with rows of Waterford crystal chandeliers. In the morning a white-hatted chef presides here over a buffet breakfast, though if you wish waitresses will serve you instead.

The bedrooms with the finest views are those at the corner of the castle overlooking both river and lake, and at the very top under the eaves, though there are larger, grander rooms elsewhere. Mine was on the ground floor, and very big. Modern reproduction furniture is gradually being replaced with antiques.

For those wanting a convivial evening, the hotel has the Dungeon Bar downstairs with its own songbook of well-known Irish songs, and live entertainment every night. Those dining will not be disappointed: during my stay, melon in a strawberry coulis, stilton and celery soup, veal cordon bleu, and apple pie were all excellent; service was swift and friendly. Ashford Castle pampers and indulges its fortunate guests.

The gourmet dining room (opposite) serves excellent seafood (above). Overleaf is a view of the lake from a turret (left). A fountain plays in the gardens (right, above); the panelled inner hall leads to the dining rooms (right, below).

ASHFORD CASTLE, Cong, Co. Mayo. **Tel.** Cong (092) 46003. **Telex** 53749 ASHC EI. **Fax** (092) 46003. **Owners** Ashford Hotels Ltd, New York. **Manager** Rory Murphy. **Open** All year. **Rooms** 54 double, 20 deluxe, 9 suites, all with bathroom (with wall shower), TV, direct-dial phone, minibar, radio, hairdryer, trouser press, piped video, iron. **Facilities** Drawing room, gourmet restaurant, dining room, Dungeon Bar, conference facilities, elevator, lake and river, own tennis, shooting, riding, jaunting cars, lake cruiser. Helicopter landing. Sight-seeing tours by arrangement. **Lunch** Yes. **Restrictions** No pets. **Terms** Deluxe (reductions out of season). **Credit cards** All major cards.

Getting there N4 to Kinnegad, N6 to Galway, Headfor Road for 27 miles to Cong. Hotel signposted (160 miles, 4 hrs). **Nearest airport** Shannon (85 miles). **Nearest rail station** Galway. **Of local interest** Cong village; Cong Abbey ruins; local walks; Lough Corrib (second largest lake in Ireland); Ross Abbey ruins. **Whole day expeditions** Connemara (Clifden and coastal villages). **Refreshments** Local pubs (ask hotel); The Red Door, Ballinrobe. **Dining out** Westwood Restaurant, Newcastle, Galway; Cashel House, Cashel (see p. 21); Enniscoe House, Castlehill (by arrangement only, see p. 11).

4 Cashel House Hotel

Presidential hideaway

Driving to Cashel House – be sure that you come to the right Cashel, see page 49 – I passed through wildly beautiful Connemara scenery, where sweeping slopes of boulder-strewn mountains are inhabited by picturesque groups of long-maned ponies and scattered with white-washed, gray-tiled cottages. The road leads down to the deeply indented bays of the rocky coast, sheltered by innumerable islands. It had been a long drive, and I hoped that a hotel in such a remote spot would prove to have been worth the journey. It was a delight.

Dermot and Kay McEvilly have won prizes both for their hotel and for their flower-filled gardens. They are splendid hosts, who welcome guests warmly and look sorry to see them go. Kay comes round during meals to see if everybody has what they need and to offer second helpings of Dermot's excellent food, which includes local sea-food and home-grown vegetables. I was not surprised to hear that many of their guests were making a second or third visit.

The comfortable, 19th-century house has log and peat fires burning in every hearth, plump inviting armchairs and plenty of magazines and books. To the large drawing room, hall-sitting room, den, and library, Dermot and Kay have added a large bar with a glass porch, where guests assemble before dinner to chat and study the promising menu, and a restaurant, also with big glass windows looking out into a small woodland glade. The bedrooms in the original house are all of different sizes, and include some charming tiny single rooms. Additional large bedrooms, built on the back of the house, overlook the pretty sloping garden and have good tiled bathrooms and big antique wardrobes. Each is pleasantly furnished with both a double and a single bed, and divided by a step and archway from a sitting area with a table, armchairs, and a further divan couch.

Although the house is only yards from the sea and has its own small beach, do not come expecting sea views, as there is a tall bank of sheltering trees between the sea and the hotel.

Dinner was exceptional. Dermot's home-smoked salmon in generous slices, tasty carrot soup, and melon sorbet were followed by a vast steamed lobster with drawn butter, accompanied by a salad mixed at the table. Rhubarb tart, a board of Irish cheeses in prime condition, and Irish coffee completed the meal. Visitors wishing to eat more lightly may do so from an *à la carte* menu.

There are walks up the hillside and along the beach, and the hotel has its own ponies and tennis court. This friendly Relais et Châteaux hotel is the perfect place to relax: no wonder the late President of France General Charles de Gaulle and his wife chose it for a fortnight's holiday.

Cosy interiors look out over the attractive gardens (opposite, above); a corner of one of the comfortable bedrooms appears above. Home-baked and home-grown produce are the basis of the excellent cuisine (opposite, below).

CASHEL HOUSE HOTEL, Cashel, Co. Galway. **Tel.** Cashel (095) 31001. **Telex** No. **Fax** No. **Owners** Dermot and Kay McEvilly. **Open** March–Nov. **Rooms** 13 suites, 16 double, 3 single, all with bathroom (30 with hand shower), direct-dial phone (TV on request in suites). **Facilities** Drawing room, bar, TV room, library, restaurant, gardens, grounds, tennis court, small private beach, rowboat, riding, mountain walks from hotel, helicopter landing, fishing (seatrout, salmon), by arrangement. **Lunch** Yes. **Restrictions** Dogs by arrangement only; no children under 5. **Terms** Expensive. **Credit cards** All major cards. **Getting there** N6, N59, turn off L to Cashel (173 miles, 5 hrs). **Nearest airport** Shannon (95 miles). **Nearest rail station** Galway. **Of local interest** Connemara: Clifden, Lough Corrib, Ross Abbey, Westport House; walks, rides. **Whole day expeditions** Aran Islands; The Burren. **Refreshments** Pubs in the small villages (ask hotel). **Dining out** Ashford Castle, Cong (see p. 17).

5 Currarevagh House

Peaceful pleasures

There are 365 islands and islets in Lough Corrib, it is said, and from the bedroom window at Currarevagh House they can be seen spread out across the lake, reed-fringed, waiting to be explored. You can take a boat from the boathouse down at the shore and spend a pleasant day pottering about the lake, sustained by a picnic hamper provided by the hotel. Ashford Castle is on the far bank, out of sight, a fairy-tale fantasy for those who like to be cocooned in luxury. Currarevagh is for people who prefer a comfortable but more simple life, plain home-cooked food, a day spent fishing, or walking in the 150-acre gardens and wooded grounds, and a quiet evening chatting by the fire.

The hydrangea bushes were in vivid blue bloom beside the neatly mown lawns under the trees when I drew up on the gravel forecourt after a winding scenic drive beside the lake. The front door stood invitingly open. The hall seemed dark after the sunshine outside, and the first thing I saw was an enormous tiger-skin, spreadeagled on the wall half-way up the stairs, spectacular against the dark brown and gold of the original wallpaper, unchanged since the house was built in 1846, yet looking as though it had been put up last year.

The Hodgson family had interests in mining, and homes in Galway and Wicklow. They demolished an older house closer to the lake, and built the existing one as a wedding present for a family member. It has fifteen bedrooms and a large, light-filled drawing room overlooking the lake; the dining room enjoys a view over the 30,000 acres of moorland and hillside that the family owned. It was then a bleak spot, which they set about planting and landscaping with the trees that are now in magnificent maturity. Hodgsons have lived here ever since. The original glass is in the wide windows and there is much aged pine in the wide dark corridors, which open into spacious simply-furnished bedrooms all with bathrooms and high ceilings.

Game soup and a fluffy soufflé jam omlette were good at dinner; breakfast is set out on the sideboard in country-house fashion for guests to choose whatever they please. Harry, friendly and helpful, June, pretty and elegant, are particularly pleasant hosts who are much involved with the Irish Country Houses and Restaurants Association, a collection of owner-managed establishments, many of which appear in this book. Currarevagh has the atmosphere of a house made for happy, leisurely house-parties. It is not luxurious, but it is a most comfortable place in which to relax, and from which to visit Galway's little villages and rocky coastline, and the imposing hills of Connemara.

Currarevagh and its own boathouse look out over Lough Corrib (opposite). The hydrangeas in vases in the comfortable sitting room (above) are picked from the splendid displays in the hotel's grounds.

CURRAREVAGH HOUSE, Oughterard, Co. Galway. **Tel.** Galway (091) 82312/82313. **Telex** No. **Fax** No. **Owners** Harry and June Hodgson. **Open** Easter–Oct. **Rooms** 13 double, 2 single, all with bathroom (11 with hand or wall shower). **Facilities** Drawing room, dining room, small bar in hall, gardens, wooded grounds, tennis, lake, croquet, boating, lake swimming, fishing, walking. Shooting, riding, by arrangement. Golf nearby. Helicopter landing. **Lunch** By arrangement. **Restrictions** No pets, and preferably no smoking in dining room. **Terms** Moderate (includes full breakfast). **Credit cards** No. **Getting there** N6 to Galway, N59 to Oughterard, turn R at sign for hotel in village, follow lakeside for 4 miles (159 miles, 4 hrs). **Nearest airport** Shannon (74 miles). **Nearest rail station** Galway. **Of local interest** Inchagoill Island; Aughnanure Castle. **Whole day expeditions** Connemara; Aran Islands; The Burren. **Refreshments** Small pubs in Oughterard (ask owner). **Dining out** Drimcong House, Moycullen; Ashford Castle, Cong (see p. 17).

Cosy exuberance

Only fourteen miles from Dublin, standing amid fields decoratively dotted with cows and sheep, this elegant Georgian manor suggests the richness of its interiors by the extravagant number of flower-filled hanging baskets, window-boxes, and urns which adorn its facade. The beautifully proportioned hall is filled with furniture – I counted four settees, twelve chairs and a table, two screens, and some potted palms – and the tall graceful drawing room has heavily-draped windows, masses of velvet chairs, walls hung with many pictures, and a most comprehensively stocked small bar. There are two conservatories and a vast and elegant dining room where a huge mahogany sideboard groans under massive silver dishes and cut-glass decanters. The bedrooms are equally splendid. Several have antique four-posters; mine had a canopied bed with white draperies and bedcover, a heavily ornate gilded dressing table and mirror, and a large bathroom, with bathrobe and plenty of big towels. Both rooms were close carpeted, with several pastel Chinese rugs added for good measure. The whole effect is one of cosy exuberant enjoyment – Norah Devlin, the owner, clearly couldn't resist acquiring these pieces, and has obviously delighted in using them to decorate her lovely mansion. She began by restoring a nearby castle hotel, which a visiting pop-star insisted on buying from her. She then bought this former dower house of the Dukes of Leinster and spent a year restoring it to its present immaculate state. Lawns outside are smoothly mown, the long drive is edged with white-painted stones.

Arriving here on a rainy day for a preliminary inspection (unknown to the owners), I was welcomed in, assured that it would be no trouble at all to make me some tea, a slice of chocolate cake was added to the tray to sustain me, and I was shown round with pride.

Returning – still not revealing my purpose in staying – I was again cherished, and had an excellent meal of cold cucumber soup, a savory pancake stuffed with mushrooms, a lemon sorbet, trout served with delicious red cabbage, and a caramel custard with wild raspberries. Portions were generous, cream lavishly used; light eaters may prefer an alternative *à la carte* menu. Coffee was served by the drawing room fire. I had an excellent night and woke to birdsong and peaceful meadow views.

County Kildare is well-known for its racehorses. There is a stud farm next door to Moyglare Manor, and about an hour's drive away is the Curragh, with its famous race track, and the National Stud, which can be visited, as can its famous Japanese Garden. On this side of Dublin you are well-placed either to drive quickly into the city, or easily to reach a main road to take you anywhere in Ireland.

Moyglare's richly furnished interiors are memorable: opposite is the entrance hall (above) and the dining room. The view from the hotel, across neighboring fields, is shown above; overleaf are the stairs and a corner of the gardens.

MOYGLARE MANOR, Maynooth, Co. Kildare. **Tel.** Dublin (01) 286351. **Telex** No. **Fax** No. **Owner** Mrs Norah Devlin. **Manager** Shay Curran. **Open** All year (except over Christmas). **Rooms** 10 double, 1 single, 3 suites, all with bathroom (12 with hand shower), direct-dial phone. TV by arrangement. **Facilities** Drawing room, bar, sitting room, restaurant, cellar sitting room, conference facilities, gardens and grounds; tennis, golf, fishing, riding, shooting by arrangement. **Lunch** Yes. **Restrictions** Children under 12 not catered for. **Terms** Expensive (includes full breakfast). **Credit cards** All major cards. **Getting there** N4 (15 miles, 30 mins). 150 miles from Shannon. **Nearest airport** Dublin. **Nearest rail station** Maynooth. **Of local interest** Castletown House (headquarters of Irish Georgian Society, fine Palladian mansion); Dublin. **Whole day expeditions** Russborough House (art collection); The Curragh (National Stud, Japanese Garden, Irish Horse Museum); Castledermot (early Christian site, Romanesque doorways). **Refreshments/Dining out** Local pubs and Dublin restaurants.

In the heart of Dublin

St Stephen's Green, with its trees and lake, is the largest garden square in Europe, and is the leafy heart of Georgian Dublin. The Shelbourne, which first opened its doors in 1824, faces the Green. James Joyce and William Makepeace Thackeray wrote about it, U.S. President Grant and his retinue stayed here, and the Irish Constitution was drafted in 1922 in an upstairs suite, which is still used today for private meetings.

The Shelbourne's present building, which dates from 1865–7, is imposing. Its vast entrance hall is adorned with black marble pillars, a heavily ornate plasterwork ceiling, an enormous chandelier, palm trees, flowers, and a porters' mahogany desk. The reception rooms are of palatial distinction and proportions, but the hotel itself is in no way forbidding. As you arrive, friendly porters hurry forward to help with baggage, and garage your car, and the well-groomed girls at the long modern reception desk tucked away at the back of the hall are efficient and helpful. There is a beauty shop, a boutique, and a same-day laundry service; tickets for the world-famous Abbey Theatre will be arranged, hire-cars or limousines organized. The Horseshoe Bar, with dark green walls and a lofty ceiling with gilded medallions, and the Lord Mayor's Lounge, a magnificent drawing room serving light luncheons, afternoon teas, and evening cocktails, have for years been meeting places for fashionable Dubliners. The Aisling Restaurant, named for a famous Edwardian socialite, Catherine O'Reilly, known as "Aisling" ("The Muse"), whose 1914 portrait hangs in the foyer, has its original cornice and splendid Waterford chandeliers. The stairs, with fine wrought-iron balustrades, lead majestically upwards to an ornate pillared landing.

Given the busy traffic swirling round St Stephen's Green, those seeking a quiet night's sleep do well to request a room or suite at the back of the hotel. Though the view will be over a service yard, the rooms are quiet. Rooms in the older part of the hotel have higher ceilings and more character: bathrooms are spacious, and the decor is appealing. My bedroom had a color scheme of blue and terracotta, with a six-foot-wide canopied bed, a spacious clothes closet and a large desk with a brass lamp. The hotel is being refurbished, so request a room which has already been redecorated.

Dinner was good, and served with professional polish: a well-seasoned pâté, fresh salmon, and a gâteau from a well-laden trolley. Outside the hotel is a taxi-rank, and a good selection of speciality boutiques. Dublin's finest Georgian streets and sights are mostly within walking distance, as are its best gourmet restaurants. Historic, majestic, the Shelbourne is conveniently placed for a visit to Dublin.

The front of The Shelbourne looks onto St Stephen's Green (opposite); above is a view of the foyer. Overleaf: left, a mirrored landing on the stairs; right, one of the fashionable afternoon teas.

THE SHELBOURNE, 27 St Stephen's Green, Dublin 2. Tel. Dublin (01) 766471. **Telex** 93653. **Fax** (01) 616006. **Owners** Trust House Forte. **Executive director** Gerald Lawless. **Open** All year. **Rooms** 146 double, 26 single, 11 junior suites, 2 two-bedroom suites, all with bathroom (with shower), TV, direct-dial phone, minibar, radio, hairdryer, own secure parking. **Facilities** Drawing room, restaurant, bar, elevator, boutique, barber, beauty shop, same-day laundry, babysitting, 24-hour room service, large conference facilities. **Lunch** Yes. **Restrictions** Small children and pets at management's discretion. **Terms** Deluxe.

Credit cards All major cards. **Getting there** Dublin is 140 miles from Shannon. **Nearest airport/rail station** Dublin. **Of local interest** Georgian Dublin; Trinity College; Mansion House; Dublin Castle; Phoenix Park; Kilmainham Hospital; Howth village; Bray village. **Whole day expedition** Glendalough monastic museum; coastal villages to the south; archaeological sites in Boyne valley. **Refreshments** Larry Murphys; The Bailey; Davy Byrnes; Toners; The Brazen Head, all in Dublin. **Dining out** Ernies; Le Coq Hardi; Whites on the Green; Patrick Guilbaud; Grey Door, all in Dublin.

Country hospitality

Those who wish to come to Ireland to ride, or to go fox-hunting or rough shooting, or just to enjoy good food in an agreeable, characterful setting should come to Ballycormac House. Although Rosetta-Anne Paxman is the eldest daughter of Lord Rathavan, and Dromoland Castle was her grandmother's home (see page 53), do not come expecting that she and her husband, John – now retired from an overseas military career – live in a stately mansion. They found this 300-year-old tiny cottage and farmyard as a dilapidated wreck, and restored it themselves, fitting everything in to the tiny rooms with great ingenuity and taste. Bathtubs are tucked into unexpected corners, sometimes boxed in with pine. Tack for the horses hangs neatly on pegs in the hall (once the kitchen), there is a little sitting room with stairs up, a peat fire burning in the grate, and just enough space for the evening's guests to fit in cosily for an after-dinner chat. Bedrooms, on the ground floor, or snugly under the eaves, are furnished with fresh, flowery fabrics and duvet-comforters, and nooks and crannies have interesting embellishments – a mounted fallow-deer head, a stuffed owl.

Everything works with a deceptively casual air and great efficiency. The lives of the Paxmans' three small children are interwoven with guests' comings and goings. A family of fluffy kittens wanders in from the stables; a Texan couple set off for a day's ride with John, big Irish hunters clopping out of the yard; two young French TV producers set out happily for a day's trout fishing; a Belgian banker drives off to Dublin; Cordon-Bleu trained Rosetta-Anne bakes a chocolate cake for tea-time. Each night a delicious dinner complete with candles is set out on a communal table; guests serve themselves from a sideboard and the girls who help with everything

clear plates and change glasses. John serves the wine and guests chat happily together.

Although not himself a fisherman, John has discovered the best places locally for fishing. He organizes rough shooting over 10,000 acres (hare, duck, pigeons, woodcock, snipe, and rabbits), and every other week he takes out a string of riders on a "progressive" four-day 150-mile ride round the northern shore of Lough Derg. After tacking-up themselves, they set off, have a picnic lunch, and are brought home by mini-bus. The horses remain to be rejoined by the riders each morning. Motorists happily explore this very pretty area, and are directed to picturesque pubs for lunch. The Paxmans are extremely nice and extremely busy (so do not expect them to linger on late at night). Staying here is like a cross between a holiday in a mountain chalet or on a boat: a happy *esprit de corps*, but with all the comforts of home.

Comfortable armchairs in the snug sitting room (opposite, below) are welcomed by guests who have spent a day out riding. The front door appears opposite, above. A horse is shod in the stableyard, above.

BALLYCORMAC HOUSE, Aglish, nr Borrisokane, Co. Tipperary. **Tel.** Nenagh (067) 21129. **Telex** 60843 (attn. Paxman. **Fax** No. **Owner** John and Rosetta-Anne Paxman. **Open** All year, except over Christmas. **Rooms** 4 double, 1 single, all with bathrooms. **Facilities** 2 sitting rooms, dining room, drying room, own riding (incl. all-in week's gourmet and riding holiday in summer), rough-shooting (incl. all-in week's shooting holiday, with guide and all meals), fishing nearby (ghillies available), hosted fox hunting in winter, helicopter landing. **Lunch** Picnic lunches only. **Restrictions** Pets by arrangement only. **Terms** Moderate (includes full breakfast). **Credit cards** All major cards. **Getting there** N7 to Roscrea, R491 to Shinrone, follow signs to Ballingarry and Aglish – also spelled Eglish (110 miles, 3 hrs). **Nearest airport** Shannon (45 miles). **Nearest rail station** Nenagh. **Of local interest** Birr Castle gardens; Lough Derg; Nenagh and Roscrea Heritage Centers; Terryglass (prizewinning village); Oldcourt, Redwood, and Lorra Castles. **Whole day expeditions** Galway via Oyster Bar, nr Oranmore, and home via Cliffs of Moher and Ennis; circuit of Lough Derg. **Refreshments** Paddy's Bar, Terryglass; Golden Pheasant, Carrigahurig. **Dining out** Gurthalougha House, Ballinderry (see p. 35).

Beside Lough Derg

There is a delightful air of peace and calm about this rambling 1840s house on the banks of Lough Derg, and this, together with Michael Wilkinson's cooking and his wife Bessie's kindly welcome, attracts devotees.

Gurthalougha House enjoys a lake view, and for guests there are boats and wind-surfers waiting at the small jetty where the kingfishers dart. Badgers can be watched in the 150 acres of woodland, and red squirrels play in the nut trees beside the house. Arriving at about lunchtime, I was brought a tray with a bowl of splendid chunky vegetable soup based on good stock, newly-baked brown bread, shortbread, and coffee in front of the drawing room fire, and sat chatting to Bessie. I noticed a man riding across the lawn: "That will be our neighbor coming in to pay his last night's dinner bill," she said. Many of their guests arrive by boat, since Lough Derg is linked to several other loughs, and – by way of locks – the sea. They tie up at the jetty, and stroll up to the house between guests playing croquet on the lawn.

Acquiring the house, fortunately in good repair, but with no furniture, the Wilkinsons spent any time left over from caring for guests and raising their children in hunting down settees and tables, mirrors and paintings. The result is an eclectic mix of the antique, the ordinary, the practical, and the irresistible – there is a four-foot carved black elephant standing in the entrance porch (most people use the back courtyard so that parked cars will not spoil the view of the lake). All the rooms are large; my bedroom overlooking the lake had twin beds with dark-green duvet-comforters, a fitted pale green carpet, good dressing table and mirror, and a slightly elderly pink velvet chair. Bessie sighed over the shabbiness of some of the carpets and furniture and rejoiced that this year they were able to re-cover their drawing room chairs in cream linen. She plans refurbishments throughout when finances allow – bathrooms came first.

You may dress as you please for dinner, candlelit at small polished tables – suit and tie, open-neck shirt (yachtsmen wear shorts and sweaters); Bessie changes from jeans to a pretty skirt. My warm chicken-liver and pistachio salad, monkfish, garden vegetables, and upside-down peach and nectarine cake with home-made icecream were served on pretty blue and white Spode china; all was delicious. The Wilkinsons have their own chickens, geese, guinea fowl, sheep, a developing vegetable garden, and fish from the lake and river. When I asked when breakfast ended, Bessie was shocked. 'Just come down any time before mid-day – or would you like breakfast in bed?' Impressed, I enquired whether guests ever abused such rule-free care, and she admitted that it had been known. "But most are marvellous, they relax here and we spoil them, that's what Gurthalougha's for."

The house looks over peaceful Lough Derg (above). At the back is a courtyard (opposite, above); the rooms are pleasantly furnished and the grounds most attractive (opposite, below).

GURTHALOUGHA HOUSE, Ballinderry, Nenagh, Co. Tipperary. **Tel.** Nenagh (067) 22080. **Telex** No. **Fax** No. **Owners** Michael and Bessie Wilkinson. **Open** All year, except 1 week over Christmas. **Rooms** 8 double, all with bathroom (1 with hand shower, 2 with wall shower). **Facilities** Drawing room, dining room, library, gardens, croquet, 150-acre woodland and nature reserve, fishing in lake and river (ghillies by arrangement), own boats and windsurfers. No shooting in grounds, but by arrangement on lake islands. Tennis planned. Helicopter landing. Language school and riding nearby. **Lunch** Snacks, by arrangement. **Restrictions** No children under 10 in dining room. **Terms** Moderate (includes full breakfast). **Credit cards** Access, Visa. **Getting there** N7 to Roscrea, then cross-country via Shinrone, Borrisokane, Ballinderry (111 miles, 3 hrs). **Nearest airport** Shannon (54 miles). **Nearest rail station** Nenagh. **Of local interest** Birr Castle and gardens; Terryglass (church, castle, pottery, craft shop). **Whole day expeditions** The Burren; Cliffs of Moher; Bunratty Folk Park. **Refreshments** Elsie Hogan's, Ballinderry; Paddy's Bar, Terryglass; The Hibernian Inn and Country Choice, Nenagh; Brocka on the Water and The Foxes' Den (both nearby). **Dining out** Ballycormac House, Aglish (by arrangement only, see p. 33).

A mansion restored

William Power, a builder, lived in Dublin, and had a business in Wicklow. Tiring of the journey to and fro he suggested to his wife Bee that they should move to Wicklow. "Only if you buy me a larger house," she replied, so he bought Tinakilly House, a huge, then-dilapidated fourteen-bedroom mansion in Rathnew, just outside Wicklow. With the help of his building firm, he totally refurbished the house, after which the logical thing seemed to be to open it as a hotel. It proved successful and the Powers are now full-time hoteliers. Bee bakes the brown bread, William welcomes the guests, takes dinner orders, and organizes the staff, who come over each year from a French catering college to help the local girls. The Powers employ a talented chef who bases the menu on fresh local produce, such as salmon, shellfish, and Wicklow lamb.

Tinakilly House stands at the end of a wide tree-lined drive, on a commanding site amid green lawns and lovely mature trees. It overlooks a tidal lake, which is a bird sanctuary, and the sea. There is a tennis court, a rapidly developing vegetable garden, and an ornamental pond with twin decorative fountains. The house was built in 1868 by Captain Halpin, a Wicklow man, who sailed before the mast first in colliers, then in clipper ships. He was a blockade runner in the American Civil War on the Confederate side before becoming captain of *The Great Eastern*. This ship, when it was launched in 1859, was the biggest in the world. From it he laid transatlantic telephone cables which remained in use until replaced by today's satellites. When Halpin retired, a grateful British Government awarded him the money to build Tinakilly House.

Inside, a grand staircase rises from the enormous hall, where a fire burns brightly in a large grate. Vast panelled rooms furnished in heavy Victoriana open from this central core: three inter-connecting dining rooms, used separately or opened into one for parties, a well-stocked bar, with massive, elaborately carved armchairs and views out to sea, and a smaller sitting room. Opposite the entrance to the sitting room hang the original plans of the house, virtually unchanged today except for a much larger kitchen. The main bedrooms are spacious, with period furniture. I stayed in a smaller bedroom, tucked cosily under the eaves, with apricot-colored furnishings, a canopied bed, and a view over the sea. All the rooms are well-equipped with telephones, televisions, and modern bathrooms (with bathrobes).

Tinakilly is a house of great character, strongly stamped with the personality of its first owner, whose photograph is on the reception desk, and whose descendants sometimes come to stay. Close to Dublin, it is convenient for small conferences, and a most agreeable stopping-place for weary travelers.

The bedrooms are comfortable and well-equipped, and a fire burns brightly in the entrance hall (opposite). The stately house (above) looks over gardens, of which two details appear overleaf (left), together with the view from one of the windows (right).

TINAKILLY HOUSE, Rathnew, Co. Wicklow. **Tel.** Wicklow (0404) 69274. **Fax** (0404) 67806. **Owners** William and Bee Power. **Open** All year. **Rooms** 14 double, incl. 1 suite, all with bathroom, TV, direct-dial phone, tea/coffee making facilities, trouser press, hairdryer. **Facilities** Drawing room/hall, sitting room, 3 dining rooms, bar, gardens and grounds, tennis. Helicopter landing. Fishing, shooting, riding, golf nearby, by arrangement. **Lunch** Yes. **Restrictions** No children under 7, no dogs. **Terms** Expensive (full breakfast included). **Credit cards** All major cards. **Getting there** N11 (25 miles, 1 hr). 145 miles from Shannon. **Nearest airport** Dublin. **Nearest rail station** Wicklow. **Of local interest** Gardens at Mount Usher and Powerscourt; Wicklow Mountains; Glendalough monastic museum; Russborough House (art collection). **Whole day expeditions** Dublin; coastal villages; Waterford (crystal factory); Wexford (music festival in Oct.); Kildare National Stud and Japanese Gardens. **Refreshments** Hunter's Hotel, Rathnew, esp. for afternoon teas (see p. 41); little local pubs (ask owner). **Dining out** Marlfield House, Gorey (see p. 43).

11 Hunter's Hotel

A long tradition of Irish hospitality

Beside the now little-traveled old coaching road from Dublin to Wicklow, which still winds and twists through wooded countryside, stands Hunter's Hotel. It has been here since the 1720s, and it has always been an inn. A cobbled entrance leads to a graceful Georgian doorway, and into a red-and-black tiled hall, worn by the feet of travelers, and polished to a high gloss. A creaking staircase leads up to a wide landing, decorated with painted china basins and ewers, once in daily use. In the hall hangs a pair of enormous ox horns, brought home by a relative from the Boer War.

Mrs Maureen Gelletlie, the fourth generation Hunter to own the inn, inherited it from her aunt, and the fifth Hunter generation, her sons Richard and Tom, trained hoteliers, already work with her. She remembers as a girl that the large pump still in the stable yard was then in use, the inn had its own cow, and hens nested in special holes in the courtyard wall. Many of their guests were families on leave from abroad, often from India. Before that time stage-coaches must once have clattered in under the archway to the stables, barns, and large walled paddock which are still there today. Their tired passengers may well have found the same kind welcome, and been whisked up to their rooms in the same brisk, bustling no-nonsense way.

Bedrooms are small and simple, with plain furniture, pretty flowered wallpaper, and gleaming tiled bathrooms. Mine looked straight out into the branches of a huge flowering magnolia, and was snug and neat. The bar is large and full of light, a pleasant place to sit and chat over a drink or a snack. It overlooks the hotel's glorious prize-winning gardens, in which flower beds and velvety lawns lead down to the river, overhung with big trees. In the bar hangs a turn-of-the-century photograph of an uncle of the owner, showing him proudly leading the Prince of Wales's horse, which he had trained, and which had just won the Grand National at Aintree. The restaurant has a low beamed ceiling, and is always busy, since local people as well as hotel guests enjoy the excellent home-cooking. Bowls of vegetables from the inn garden are put on the table for you to serve yourself, there are hearty old-fashioned puddings, and the menu changes daily.

It is rare to find a hotel which is in such lovely surroundings, with such a feeling of a continuing tradition of hospitality.

Hunter's Hotel is famous for its prize-winning gardens (opposite, above). Guests can enjoy a glass of Guinness in the bar before dinner in the restaurant (opposite, below). A detail of the landing is shown above.

HUNTER'S HOTEL, Rathnew, Co. Wicklow. **Tel.** Rathnew (0404) 40106. **Telex** No. **Fax** No. **Owner** Mrs Maureen Gelletlie. **Open** All year. **Rooms** 12 double, 5 single, 10 with ensuite bathrooms. **Facilities** Sitting room, restaurant, bar, TV room, large gardens with river, small conference facilities. River and sea fishing and riding locally, by arrangement. **Lunch** Yes. **Restrictions** No pets in public rooms. **Terms** Moderate (includes full breakfast). **Credit cards** All major cards. **Getting there** N11 (28 miles, 1 hr). 150 miles from Shannon. **Nearest airport** Dublin. **Nearest rail station** Wicklow. **Of local interest** Gardens at Mount Usher and Powerscourt; Russborough House; Avondale. **Whole day expeditions** Wicklow Mountains; Glendalough (monastic ruins and museum); Dublin. **Refreshments** Tinakilly House, Rathnew (see p. 37). **Dining out** Marlfield House, Gorey (see p. 43).

12 Marlfield House

Gourmets' delight

I came to Marlfield House, once the residence of the Earls of Courtown, with high expectations, for it had been warmly recommended to me by several friends. I was not disappointed. An elaborate glass entrance porch housing an antique reception desk has been added to the formerly rather plain Regency stone facade, and this leads through to an inner hall, bright with fresh flowers. From here a graceful staircase curls steeply upwards, hung with portraits, and lit at each level by progressively larger glittering Waterford crystal chandeliers, all linked to one central chain. On the right is a huge and gracious drawing room, with a well-stock mahogany bar in one corner. Furnished with dark blue wallpaper, an Alice-through-the-Looking-Glass mirror, and a gilded clock, it has an open fire and a big oil painting of a fetchingly wistful Edwardian Countess. Tall French windows lead from here into the restaurant. A second smaller sitting room is filled with excellent antiques, and there is a library for the use of residents only.

The restaurant is justly famous. At the back of the house, it is a spectacular conservatory, filled with green plants and flower-filled hanging baskets. An inner mirrored section reflects painted forest scenes, and is snug in winter; an outer section opens to the garden for summer dining. The view is of well-tended green lawns, huge trees, rose beds, neat gravel paths, bright herbaceous borders, and a clipped hedge behind which are vast vegetable gardens, the pride of owners Raymond and Mary Bowe. The impeccable dinner was served on delicate Wedgwood china laid on starched white damask cloths. I began with tasty sweetbreads in a light mushroom and white wine sauce, followed by a seasonal salad with a tangy dressing, and a velvet-smooth grape sorbet. New

season's lamb was rubbed with garlic and served pink with a basil sauce, and the vegetables were freshly gathered from the garden. A light strawberry shortcake and petits fours completed one of the best meals I have eaten in Ireland. Breakfast next morning in the sunlit conservatory was equally memorable.

My bedroom, at the top of the house, was made well worth the climb by the view. It had a four-poster bed, draped with ruffled glazed chintz patterned with fat pink roses, green velvet armchairs, an antique walnut tallboy, and a tiled bathroom with a good shower and gold taps. There are ground-floor bedrooms for those not wishing to tackle the stairs. Mary Bowe has a passion for antiques, and has added extra bedrooms to house the fine pieces she has collected. Connoisseurs of country house hotels will find it well worth making the journey to Ireland to stay in this welcoming gourmet retreat.

Shown opposite are one of the bedrooms, the entrance hall, and coffee in the garden; above is a mouth-watering plate of oysters and overleaf are views of the conservatory restaurant (left) and the drawing room (right).

MARLFIELD HOUSE, Gorey, Co. Wexford. **Tel.** Gorey (055) 21124. **Telex** 054 80757. **Fax** (055) 21572. **Owners** Mary and Raymond Bowe. **Open** 1 Feb.–31 Dec., and New Year. **Rooms** 11 double, 2 single, 6 suites, all with bathroom (incl. wall shower), TV, direct-dial phone. **Facilities** Drawing room/bar, sitting room, library, restaurant, grass tennis court, croquet, gardens, grounds. Helicopter landing. 1 mile to golf club and sandy beach; fishing, riding, shooting, hunting, by arrangement. **Lunch** Yes. **Restrictions** Pets and young children only by prior arrangement with management. **Credit cards** All major cards. **Terms** Expensive (includes full breakfast). **Getting**

there N11 to Gorey. In Gorey, turn L just before railway bridge, hotel 1 mile along Courtown rd on R (58 miles, about 1½ hrs). 200 miles from Shannon. **Nearest airport** Dublin. **Nearest rail station** Gorey. **Of local interest** Wicklow; coastal villages; gardens of Mount Usher and Powerscourt; Glendalough (early Christian monastic ruins and museum). **Whole day expeditions** Dublin; Russborough House (art collection, including paintings by Goya, Rubens, Velasquez; silver; gardens); Blessington; Wicklow mountains; Rothe House; Kilkenny. **Refreshments** Little local pubs, ask hotel. **Dining out** Nothing nearby.

13 Clohamon House

A gracious family welcome

Sir Richard and Lady Levinge live in what was once the family's home for fishing holidays, an attractive 1780s house in a glorious situation overlooking the Slaney river. Sheltered by huge trees in 180 acres, it is edged with a neat garden which is the pride of Lady Levinge, since she has won much of it back from a wilderness, while her husband has been improving the home farm. She runs her own Connemara pony stud farm on the premises, and travels widely to international horse shows, both to act as a judge and to show her own ponies. There are herons and wild duck on the flight pond below the house, badgers in the woods nearby, and a glorious panoramic view of Mount Leinster directly in front of the house.

Portraits of the Levinges through the centuries hang on the drawing room walls, and there are fine Flemish tapestries in the dining room, where at dinner and breakfast guests sit at a long polished table set with family silver. They will not be joined at their meals by their hosts, except perhaps for coffee, since Lady Levinge is the talented self-taught cook who produces the excellent meals. On my visit I enjoyed her crisp courgettes in a light batter, with a stilton, yoghurt, and fresh-peppercorn sauce. Equally delicious were the celery and apple soup, lamb cutlets from the Levinges' own farm with vegetables from the garden, and home-made Bailey's Irish liqueur icecream, sprinkled with toasted almonds. There was local farm cheese, in a state of perfect ripeness, and fresh chocolate truffles with the coffee, served from a silver pot by the fireside. Sir Richard, tall and blond, appeared briefly, on his way to another farm. He sometimes takes over preparation of breakfast. Eggs are free-range, sausages are made locally, the brown bread is freshly baked, and preserves home-made. Their young children enjoy chatting with the guests, when on holiday from their boarding schools.

On the stairs hangs a portrait of a very determined-looking lady, the mother of the poet Edward FitzGerald (who translated the *Rubáiyát* of Omar Khayyám). Lady Levinge's mother was a FitzGerald, her father Prince d'Ardia Caracciolo, and she herself was born at Waterford Castle (see page 91) and is a distant relative of The Knight of Glin (see page 55). My bedroom overlooked the glorious view and was furnished with family antiques. There were plenty of books and magazines, a good bed, many thoughtful extras, and an ensuite bathroom with shampoo and big soft towels. Remember that since this is a family house, you must have booked well in advance. Clohamon House is a gracious and comfortable place to visit, and has welcoming and hospitable owners.

The comfortable sitting room and gracious formal dining room are shown opposite; both are furnished with the family's antiques. Lady Levinge's Connemara ponies graze outside the house (above).

CLOHAMON HOUSE, Bunclody, Co. Wexford. **Tel.** Enniscorthy (054) 77253. **Telex** No. **Fax** No. **Owners** Sir Richard and Lady Levinge. **Open** 1 March–1 Nov. At other times by special arrangement only, for hunting, etc. **Rooms** 3 double, 1 single, 2 with ensuite bathroom (incl. wall shower), 2 with ensuite shower-room. Hairdryers and cordless phone available. **Facilities** Drawing room, dining room, 180-acre parkland, pastures, gardens, river with own fishing. Helicopter landing. Clay pigeon shooting, walks in grounds, Connemara pony stud, farm, badger-watching. Stabling for guests' horses. Riding/hunting (6 packs), hang-gliding, and golf nearby, by arrangement. Hill-walking, canoeing. **Lunch** No. **Restrictions** Dogs by arrangement only. **Terms** Moderate (includes full breakfast); children sharing rooms charged half-price. **Credit cards** Visa. **Getting there** Via Naas (N7), L on N9 to Castledermot, R on R418 to Tullow, R on N81/N80 to Bunclody; follow signs from market square. Or via N11 to Gorey and Ferns, R on R745, R again on N80 and ask (70 miles, 2 hrs). 90 miles from Shannon. **Nearest airport** Dublin. **Nearest rail station** Enniscorthy. **Of local interest** Clonegal village; Huntington Castle; Altamont Gardens. **Whole day expeditions** Saltee Island (bird watching); Irish National Stud at Kilkenny; Russborough House (art collection); Waterford (crystal factory); Wexford Opera Festival in October; horse-racing at Wexford and Gowran; greyhound racing at Enniscorthy. **Refreshments** Local pubs (ask owners). **Dining out** Marlfield House, Gorey (see p. 43).

Cashel
Co. Tipperary

In an Archbishop's Palace

There are two points to remember if planning a visit to Cashel Palace: be sure to arrive at the right Cashel (since there is another one, on the west coast, also with an excellent hotel: see page 21), and to have reserved a room at the back overlooking the castle ruins which, floodlit at night, are spectacular.

In the middle of the small town, impressive gates open into a long forecourt, at the end of which is the splendid red-brick facade of this former Archbishop's Palace, built *c.* 1731 and designed by Sir Edward Lovett Pearce, architect of the old Parliament House in Dublin. I had wondered whether a town setting would prove noisy, but the hotel is set well back from the traffic in a peaceful, sheltering garden. The pillared entrance hall is imposing. Panelled in pine, painted a delicate apricot, it has twin gray-marble fireplaces facing each other, flanked by comfortable settees. Though in a lovely historic setting, this is a thoroughly professional, efficiently-run hotel, with helpful friendly girls at the reception desk. I was given the Bishop's Room, at the top of the wide, elaborately carved staircase which leads from a side hall up to a spacious long panelled landing. Other cosy, chintzy low-ceilinged bedrooms are tucked up under the eaves, but my bedroom was one of the largest I have ever seen. Lined with gathered dark pink silk, it had a lofty ceiling and central chandelier. The bathroom was simple but vast. There was an enormous bed, its high headpiece painted white and carved with garlands and flambeaux, from which green and white draperies hung down. The view, morning and evening, was magnificent: the Rock of Cashel, crowned with its ruined cathedral, castle, chapel, and tall tower, framed in the weeping ash and copper-beech trees of the neatly tended wide gardens. A pair of gnarled old mulberry trees on the smooth lawns may be even

older than the Palace, for they are said to have been planted in 1702 for Queen Anne's coronation.

Downstairs there is an attractive Garden Suite for those who wish to avoid the stairs, a large drawing room, and a high-ceilinged dining room in which I enjoyed an excellent dinner. A smooth pâté and a rich creamy bisque were followed by fresh lobster removed from its shell and served in a light sauce, and a fresh raspberry sabayon. There was a delicious selection of home-baked breads. Each table was lit by a candle in a cut-glass Waterford crystal holder; service was swift and concerned. I sat watching swallows darting about in the evening light, and rooks returning to their roosts. In the stone-flagged cellars is the Bishop's Buttery, an informal restaurant serving light meals, and a small convivial cellar bar.

I slept soundly, roused only once briefly by a cock crowing at 4.30 in the morning, and once by a vivid dream I could not remember. I asked as I was leaving if the hotel had any ghosts. "No," they said, "well, only the Bishop, in the Bishop's Room . . ."

Well-tended gardens surround this stately 18th-century mansion (opposite), which has an imposing pillared entrance hall (above). Overleaf (left) is a glimpse of the grounds; on the right is the Bishop's Room, below a view of the Rock of Cashel.

CASHEL PALACE HOTEL, Main Street, Cashel, Co. Tipperary. **Tel.** Cashel (062) 61411. **Telex** 70638. **Fax** (062) 61521. **Owner/Manager** Ray Carroll. **Open** All year. **Rooms** 15 double, 2 single, 3 suites, all with bathroom (incl. hand/wall shower), TV, radio, direct-dial phone. **Facilities** Drawing room, bar, 2 restaurants, river, gardens, private path to Rock of Cashel, conference facilities. Helicopter landing. River fishing, shooting, riding available locally, by arrangement. **Lunch** Yes. **Restrictions** No dogs. **Terms** Deluxe. **Credit cards** All major cards. **Getting there** N7/N8 (101 miles, 2 hrs). Hotel in town. **Nearest airport** Shannon (60 miles). **Nearest rail station** Thurles. **Of local interest** Rock of Cashel (12th–15th-century buildings, fine carvings); Athassel Priory; Holycross Abbey; Cahir Castle; Coolmore Stud. **Whole day expeditions** Waterford Crystal Factory; Kilkenny Castle; Blarney Castle (nr Cork); Bunratty Castle (nr Limerick). **Refreshments** Small local pubs. **Dining out** Chez Hans Restaurant, Cashel.

Historic grandeur

Conor O'Brien, 18th Baron Inchiquin, is the O'Brien of Thomond, direct descendant of Brian Boru, High King of Ireland, who defeated the Vikings at the Battle of Clontarf in 1014. He still lives amid the 1000-acre estate through which the river Rine meanders, and is the former owner of Dromoland Castle, though he has built himself a new, more modest mansion, and his erstwhile ancestral home is now a luxury hotel. You may, if you wish, stay with him on a bed-and-breakfast basis, though it is the castle which offers the greater grandeur.

The original entrance leads up into a small hall, furnished with a spreading many-armed brass candelabrum and ancestral portraits. Doors open into the former library, shelved floor to ceiling, which now contains the bar – it overlooks the lake – and a small sitting room, which has a view of the rose-garden. A wide gallery lined with antlered heads and containing groups of elegant settees ends in a straight wide flight of steps up to the main bedrooms. Beside them is a well-stocked boutique providing useful necessities – as I discovered, having inadvertently abandoned my washbag at my last stop – as well as Irish silver, knitwear, crystal, postcards, and pottery. Beyond this is the present reception hall, where guests are welcomed and where I glimpsed the hotel's amiable wolfhound, named after an Irish hero. There are smaller, pleasantly furnished rooms round a pretty courtyard in a wing to the left of the entrance (the original castle), but they can be noisy if a guest in the room above is early-rising or a night owl. I would suggest asking for a room in the main building, an 1826 fantasy on a medieval theme. The bedrooms are plain, but vary from large to enormous, and have excellent bathrooms.

Dinner was an extremely pleasant experience. The majestic dining room, rich in carvings, gilded and swagged, overlooks the lake. Starched white damask cloths, polished silver, pretty Wedgwood china, and flowers on the tables made a pleasing picture; there was even a girl singing tunefully at a harp. When my son chose this moment to phone me from San Francisco, a cordless phone was brought to me without fuss. The food was delicious: crayfish and lobster salad, a delicate consommé, and a sirloin steak with a red wine *marchand de vin* sauce. A rich chocolate dessert with an apricot coulis was followed by delicate petits fours with the coffee.

Viewed across the lake, Dromoland's wealth of crenelated battlements, towers, turrets, and flags rising from the smoothly mown green undulations of the 18-hole golf course appears almost unbelievably picturesque. This is a splendidly impressive hotel.

The castle towers over its trim rose gardens (opposite): this was once the main entrance. The somewhat stern exterior contrasts with the elegant comfort of the interiors; one of the main corridors is shown above.

DROMOLAND CASTLE, Newmarket-on-Fergus, Co. Clare. **Tel.** Newmarket (061) 71144. **Telex** 70654. **Fax** 363355. **Owners** Ashford Hotels Ltd. **Manager** David Pantin. **Open** All year. **Rooms** 54 double, 17 suites, all with bathroom (incl. wall shower), TV, direct-dial phone, radio, room service. **Facilities** Drawing room, sitting room, bar, double dining room, boutique, large conference facilities, gardens, 1000-acre grounds with river and lake, 18-hole golf course, croquet, tennis, fishing, shooting, stalking, bicycling. Helicopter landing. Riding by arrangement. **Lunch** Yes. **Restrictions** None. **Terms** Deluxe. **Credit cards** All major cards. **Getting there** N7 to Limerick, then N18 (125 miles, 4 hrs). **Nearest airport** Shannon (9 miles). **Nearest rail station** Ennis. **Of local interest** Adare Manor and village; Bunratty Castle and Folk Park; Cliffs of Moher; The Burren; Lisdoonvarna Wells (spa and health center). **Whole day expeditions** Killarney and lakes; Dingle Peninsula; Blarney Castle; Cork; Kinsale village. **Refreshments** Dirty Nellie's, MacCloskey's, Bunratty; Brogans and Mungavons in Ennis. **Dining out** Doyle's Seafood Bar, Dingle; The Mustard Seed and Adare Manor, Adare (see p. 59).

Make a castle your home

For anyone who has ever fantasized about living in a castle, or contemplated purchasing their own, Glin Castle provides the opportunity to take over an antique-filled historic gem, with its own impeccably trained staff, and enough suites of rooms, bathrooms, and dressing rooms to allow you to organize your own house-party. An account will be opened for you with the local tradesmen, and your only exertion will be to discuss and decide menus with the self-effacing and expertly-trained ladies who have been here since the 1920s. You may also draw on produce from the home farm and gardens, after due discussion with Tom the gardener. You may stay for a week or a month, or the whole summer, but occasionally rooms in the castle may be available for those just wanting a meal, bed, and breakfast. The owners, who live in a separate wing, are frequently away, though try if possible to greet arriving guests.

Glin Castle is the ancestral home of the Knight of Glin – 29th in succession, Harvard-educated art historian, Christie's fine arts representative in Ireland, author, expert on Irish decorative art – his wife Madame Fitz-Gerald, who also writes, and their three daughters. The title dates from the 1300s, the castle from the end of the 1700s, a fine Georgian house crenelated in the 1830s by the 25th Knight. You enter through the gatehouse in the village. A high wall encircles the estate, its farm, parklands, and immaculate gardens.

The entrance hall, with classical pillars, a polished floor, and family portraits, has a superb neoclassical ceiling. All the rooms house an exceptional collection of Irish 18th-century walnut and mahogany furniture. Other fine ceilings, worthy of Adam, are in the stately drawing room, and in the bookcase-lined library. I ate in solitary splendor in the spacious dining room. The pâté and soup were exceptional, the steak tender and juicy, an apple tart melted in the mouth. Coffee was served in front of the fire in the elegant morning room. My well furnished and very comfortable bedroom had a sea view and was perfumed by a vase of sweet-scented roses from the garden.

Ambassadors, statesmen, famous musicians, or top executives accustomed to faultless service from excellent staff, and wanting to entertain privately, find this a far more civilized option than any hotel.

The splendid interiors include the drawing room (opposite, above), the Yellow Bedroom (opposite, below), and the dining room (above). Overleaf: the castle from the gardens, with the sea glimpsed behind the trees.

GLIN CASTLE, Glin, Co. Limerick. **Tel.** Glin (068) 34173. Bookings by arrangement through In the English Manner or Elegant Ireland (see p. 7). **Telex** No. **Fax** No. **Owners** The Knight of Glin and Madame Fitz-Gerald. **Open** All year. **Rooms** 4 suites: the Pink Rooms (1 double, 1 single, 1 bathroom); the Blue Rooms (2 double – 1 with four-poster – 1 single, 1 bathroom); the Yellow Rooms (1 double, 1 single, 1 bathroom); the Green Rooms (1 twin, 1 bathroom). Comfortable maximum: 8–10 people. **Facilities** Main hall, drawing room, library, morning room, dining room, 3 washrooms, kitchens, pantries, nursery, tennis court, gardens, 500-acre estate and dairy farm. Helicopter landing. Golf at Ballybunion, Lahinch, Fenit, Adare, by arrangement. **Lunch** Yes. **Restrictions** None. **Terms** Deluxe. The flat fee includes the services of a cook and 2 housekeepers, as well as utilities, but does not include the cost of food for the guests or staff. Usually let in 1–2 week periods. The more guests, the cheaper the individual cost – exceptionally expensive for 2, very good value indeed for 10. Dinner, bed, and breakfast may sometimes be available. **Credit cards** No. **Getting there** N7 to Limerick, N69 to Glin (150 miles, 4 hrs). **Nearest airport** Shannon (45 miles). **Nearest rail station** Limerick. **Of local interest** Adare; Bunratty Folk Park; Askeaton (ruins of friary); Tarbut to County Clare car ferry for Cliffs of Moher; Dingle Peninsula. **Whole day expeditions** Limerick; Ring of Kerry; Cashel; Killarney. **Refreshments** O'Shaughnessy's pub, Glin; Inn Between and Mustard Seed, Adare; Dirty Nellie's, MacCloskey's, Bunratty; Doyle's Seafood Bar, Dingle. **Dining out** Dromoland Castle, Newmarket-on-Fergus (see p. 53); Adare Manor, Adare (see p. 59); Cashel Palace, Cashel (see p. 49).

Victorian magnificence

Adare Manor is the former seat of the Earls of Dunraven, and has now become a luxurious hotel. The original 1720s house was rebuilt and enlarged by the second and third Earls between 1832 and 1860, creating a vast Victorian Gothic mansion whose inner hall, reached from a small outer foyer through gilded Spanish leather doors, soars cathedral-like in high pointed stone arches, lit by tall windows, brightened by giant arrangements of fresh flowers.

A fire burns cheerfully in the wide hearth beside the reception desk. A massive staircase winds upwards, though there is an elevator for those daunted by the long steep climb. Most of the bedrooms are on the same lordly scale; one has the family motto written in Latin in tall letters of gold round the walls. My room at the top gave me a housemartin's view of the garden – and also allowed me to peer down into their nests on a nearby ledge. The elaborately patterned flowerbeds in scarlet and gold were edged with low hedges, the river sparkled on my left, large trees rose up on the right, and ahead, beyond the shaven lawns, pastureland dotted with browsing cows stretched towards the misty blue mountains. As well as having a spectacular view, I had a 6-foot bed, pleasant reproduction furniture, a fine antique mirror, a tasteful arrangement of fresh flowers, Waterford crystal reading lamps, and a magnificent marble bathroom.

The public rooms are equally august. The Grand Gallery, well over a hundred feet long, lit by stained glass windows and furnished with a set of carved medieval choir stalls, is a distinguished setting for functions. The drawing room has groups of settees in window bays and in front of the large tiled fireplace, designed – like much of the interior – by A.W.N. Pugin, who helped to create the British Houses of Parliament. The drawing room leads at one end to a lofty bar and at the other to a panelled library which serves as an anteroom to the very grand, chandelier-hung restaurant. Friendly young waiters in long white aprons brought excellent canapés before a well-presented dinner, served on gold-and-lapis-bordered Coalport china. Duckling *en croûte*, veal with fresh vegetables, apple tartlet with calvados sauce, followed by coffee and petits fours, were all excellent. A harpist played during dinner. A convivial cellar-bar is being planned, offering live music and snacks.

At the gates of Adare Manor lies Adare village, said to be the most picturesque in Ireland. It has thatched cottages, a 13th-century church, impressive ruins, and many interesting little shops and pubs. One will never be bored in this splendid manor, surrounded by trim parkland and an 840-acre estate, a distinguished setting for a luxurious holiday.

The manor is set amid spacious grounds through which a river runs (opposite, above and below right); the book-lined library (opposite, below left) leads to the dining room. Above is one of the sumptuous bathrooms. The entrance hall (overleaf) is a splendid Victorian vision of the Middle Ages.

ADARE MANOR, Adare, Co. Limerick. **Tel.** Adare (061) 86566. **Telex** 70733 ADAR EI. **Fax** (061) 86124. **Owners** Mr and Mrs Thomas Kane. **Manager** Christopher J. Oakes. **Open** All year. **Rooms** 28 double (there will eventually be 51), incl. 2 suites and 11 state rooms, all with bathroom (incl. hand and wall shower), TV (satellite), direct-dial phone. **Facilities** Drawing room, dining room, library, 2 bars, Long Gallery, room service, conference facilities, elevator, gardens, 840-acre grounds, river with 3 miles exclusive fishing, riding by arrangement, local hunt, helicopter landing, courtesy car by arrangement. Plans include own tennis court, shooting, heated indoor pool, equestrian center. **Lunch** Yes. **Restrictions** None. **Terms** Deluxe. **Credit cards** All major cards. **Getting there** N7 to Limerick, N21 to Adare (131 miles, 4 hrs). **Nearest airport** Shannon (30 miles). **Nearest rail station** Limerick. **Of local interest** Adare (village, ruins of 15th-century Franciscan friary and 13th-century church). **Whole day expeditions** Limerick; bicycle expeditions and watersports arranged by hotel; Bunratty Folk Park; Muckross House gardens, lakes; Killarney. **Refreshments** The Inn Between, Mustard Seed, Adare; Dirty Nellie's, MacCloskey's, Bunratty. **Dining out** Dromoland Castle, Newmarket-on-Fergus (see p. 53).

18 Great Southern Hotel

Killarney
Co. Kerry

Near the Lakes of Killarney

A traditional hotel with an imposing facade, pillared entry porch at the top of a flight of steps with highly-polished brass hand-rails, and an enormous entry hall with a welcoming fire burning brightly in its marble fireplace, the Great Southern at Killarney is one of Ireland's first great railway hotels. Built in 1854, it is set back from the road at the edge of town which leads to the Ring of Kerry, a picturesque route along the edge of the Kerry Peninsula, passing through fishing villages, among Killarney's famous lakes, and over some spectacular mountain passes.

I found the Great Southern to be a hotel of many pleasant surprises. The first was that there are ten acres of well-tended gardens, invisible as you approach the hotel: hidden away at the back are bright flowerbeds, smooth lawns, walks, and woodlands stretching away to the nearby mountains. The second surprise was how quiet the bedroom was – always something to be checked with a town hotel. Most of the bedrooms overlook the gardens and the view; those in the older part of the building have high ceilings, and windows with their original shutters; the more modern wing has smaller rooms. Decor varies from the traditional to modern; there are linen sheets and soft down pillows on the beds.

My next pleasant surprise was the excellent standard of food and service. Large hotels are not always noted for their fine cuisine, or their sparkling service, and I was delighted to find that there was an excellent chef, and a helpful attentive staff. The main dining room is gigantic. Its bay-window overlooks the view and one end can be closed off for private parties. Tables are covered with well-starched damask cloths and laid with well-polished silver.

Dishes are first presented before being served. My vegetable soup, and rack of lamb with generous portions of well-cooked broccoli, cauliflower, beans, and two varieties of potato, were extremely good, as were a frothy orange mousse and coffee. There is also a small award-winning gourmet restaurant with a French menu, The Malton Room (named for its fine collection of 18th-century prints of Dublin by the noted artist James Malton).

Within strolling distance there are many shops and the famous jaunting cars whose cheerful drivers will take you on horse-drawn excursions through the National Park and beside the lakes. The hotel itself has a well-stocked boutique with Waterford glass, hand-woven tweeds, and hand-knitted Aran woolens. There is also a convivial bar and an indoor heated pool. Here are modern comforts in a pleasantly old-world setting.

The hotel enjoys a view of distant mountains across its gardens (opposite, above); excellent food is served in the attractive dining rooms. A cheerful fire burns in the entrance hall (above).

GREAT SOUTHERN HOTEL, Killarney, Co. Kerry. **Tel.** Killarney (064) 31262. **Telex** 73998. **Fax** (064) 31642. **Owners** Great Southern Hotels Ltd. **Manager** Michael Rosney. **Open** 1 March–2 Jan. **Rooms** 152 double, 6 single, 12 suites, all with bathroom (with wall shower), TV, direct-dial phone, radio, trouser press, most with hair dryers. **Facilities** Hall/drawing room, smoking room, 2 restaurants, bar, 2 elevators, room service, 10 acres of gardens and woodlands, croquet, snooker, tennis, indoor heated pool, parking, live music and theater in the evening, large conference center in garden with ballroom and meetings room. Helicopter landing. Fishing, shooting, riding, jaunting-car rides, golf by arrangement. **Terms** Expensive. Ask about seasonal reductions and special breaks. **Restrictions** None. **Credit cards** All major cards. **Getting there** N4 to Limerick, N21/N22 to Killarney (189 miles, 4 hrs). **Nearest airport** Shannon (120 miles). **Nearest rail station** 20 yards away. **Of local interest** Muckross House; Irish Transport Museum; National Folk Theater productions; National Park. **Whole day expeditions** Ring of Kerry; Dingle Peninsula; West Cork. **Refreshments** Many pubs and small restaurants within walking distance (ask hotel). **Dining out** Great Southern Hotel, Parknasilla (see p. 65); Park Hotel, Kenmare (see p. 67). Doyle's Seafood Bar, Dingle.

On the Ring of Kerry

The grandfather of poet Robert Graves rented the original house at Parknasilla as a summer residence. It was bought by Southern Hotels, who in 1890 erected a new hotel nearby, designed by the architect of the Park Hotel (see page 67) and Ashford Castle (see page 17). This was immediately bought by Great Southern Railways, who found themselves in the curious position of owning a winter resort hotel nowhere near a rail station. Their passengers had to be conveyed by horse and carriage the not inconsiderable fifteen miles from Kenmare.

Today the hotel is a summer resort, and closes in winter. It is run with efficiency and a great deal of charm, providing the expertise of a modern hotel in a setting of Victorian splendor. The view is magnificent: the bay is spread out before the hotel and is scattered with small islands – the hotel owns two, and you can walk to them over a footbridge and picnic there if you wish. There is also a little private rocky cove, hidden beside the indoor pool, where sailing boats and a motor boat for water skiing await your pleasure. There are large, well-tended grounds with palm trees, horses if you wish to ride, and a prize-winning village to explore a few miles down the road. The staff are particularly delightful – three have been here so long that they can greet by name guests they knew as children who are bringing back their own children for holidays: the head porter Tom, the barman Sonny, and the head waiter Jackie.

The hotel has been entirely refurbished and a new wing added since its Victorian heyday. Bedrooms have good modern bathrooms and are close carpeted. Furnishings are in pleasant plain shades, in no way frilly or country-house, but everywhere is spotless. A large sun-lounge sitting room provides promptly-served freshly-prepared snacks; a more formal drawing room has chandeliers and a large fireplace, where a fire is lit each evening; the dining room has sea views and pleasant peach-colored decor. The food is tasty, the service impeccable.

The Ring of Kerry on which the hotel stands is one of Ireland's most noted beauty spots. Great bushes of crimson fuchsias and clusters of orange day-lilies line the narrow road which circles the Kerry Peninsula.

Parknasilla does not have designer-chic, but it does have a finer setting and far better service and food than many places with far greater pretentions. I met an American in another very grand establishment who had visited more than forty countries and stayed in many luxury hotels, but said that he had enjoyed Parknasilla more than anywhere else, and was planning to return. He is in good company – several members of Europe's royalty have chosen Parknasilla as a place to spend their family holidays.

The sea, scattered with small islands, lies directly in front of the hotel (opposite). The porter's desk can be seen through the main entrance, above.

GREAT SOUTHERN HOTEL, Parknasilla, Co. Kerry. **Tel.** Kenmare (064) 45122. **Telex** 73899. **Fax** (064) 45323. **Owners** Great Southern Hotels Ltd. **Manager** James W. Feeney. **Open** Easter–end Oct. **Rooms** 60 double, incl. 1 large and 2 mini suites, all with bathroom (with wall shower), TV, direct-dial phone, radio. **Facilities** Drawing room, sitting room, bar, restaurant, room service, billiards, conference facilities, heated indoor pool, tennis, sea fishing, riding, shooting, 9-hole golf course, sailing, water skiing, baby-sitting, same-day laundry, dry cleaning, shoe-shining. **Lunch** Yes. **Restrictions** No pets. **Terms** Deluxe. **Credit cards** All major cards. **Getting there** N7 to Limerick, N21/N22 to Killarney, N71 to Kenmare, N70 to hotel (255 miles, 6 hrs). **Nearest airport** Shannon (120 miles). **Nearest rail station** Killarney. **Of local interest** Ring of Kerry; Sneem village; Killarney lakes. **Whole day expeditions** Garinish Island; Dingle Peninsula; Bantry House (see p. 79); Skeilig Rock (early monastic settlement, reached by boat). **Refreshments** Ask hall porter about local pubs. **Dining out** Park Hotel, Kenmare (see p. 67); Great Southern Hotel, Killarney (see p. 63).

A fashionable venue for Ireland's high society

The lake district of Killarney is a famous beauty spot, and you can choose to come to Kenmare by the road from Killarney that passes through the pretty woodlands beside the lakes, then climbs steeply up, narrow and winding, to spectacular mountain views, and down to the seashore at Kenmare.

The Park Hotel was built originally as a railway hotel in 1897, and has the sturdy gray-stone dignity of the period. It is high on a hillside, with immaculate terraced gardens and walkways leading down to fields, woods, and the tidal estuary of the Kenmare river. Its own 9-hole golf course is off to one side, bright hanging baskets of flowers are suspended from the delicate ironwork tracery of the verandah, groups of white chairs are set out invitingly on the lawn, and I arrived in time to sit and enjoy an excellent afternoon tea watching the ducks on the river, and rabbits playing in the cornfield.

The long drive curves up behind the hotel to an impressive entrance reached by a flight of steps beneath an awning. In the elegant hall hung with vast oil paintings, very correctly attired but welcoming young gentlemen greet you and invite you to sign in at an antique desk. There is a handsome antique cistern painted with mythological figures supported on gilded seahorses and dolphins, and a fire burns in a marble fireplace. You should be sure to have booked well in advance in order to have secured one of the six spacious suites, which are likewise furnished with splendid antiques, including magnificent carved beds, as the secondary bedrooms are considerably plainer and smaller.

There is a pleasant hexagonal bar with doors opening to the view. Beside it is a comfortable sitting room, where a pianist plays in the evening. The restaurant runs the length of the verandah – so many tables have the advantage of the view – and into a main room; there is a fine marble fireplace at each end. Over one is an impressive still-life of seafood, over the other a portrait in oils of a pensive lady; another huge still-life is of flowers. Chandelier and wall lights are in the shape of white translucent lilies; massive, well-polished silverware, antiques, palm trees, well-starched damask linen tablecloths, and a harpist with a very sweet voice complete the feeling of Edwardian grandeur. Dinner was well-presented by formally dressed waiters and girls in pretty flowered dresses, and based on excellent fresh produce.

This is a gracious, very professional, and highly praised hotel, owned and run by one of Ireland's leading hoteliers, Francis Brennan, and much frequented by Ireland's high society.

Woods and fields surround the hotel's gardens (opposite, above). The spacious rooms are most attractively furnished with antiques; a corner of the entrance hall is shown opposite, below; above is a bedroom in one of the suites.

PARK HOTEL KENMARE, Kenmare, Co. Kerry. **Tel.** Killarney (064) 41200. **Telex** 73905 PARK EI. **Fax** (064) 41402. **Owner/Manager** Francis Brennan. **Open** April–mid-Nov.; Christmas–New Year. **Rooms** 31 double, 12 single, 6 suites, all with bathroom (with hand shower), direct-dial phone, radio. **Facilities** Drawing room, bar, restaurant, elevator, billiards, tennis, 9-hole golf, croquet; shooting, fishing, riding, by arrangement; helicopter landing; small conference facilities. **Lunch** Yes. **Restrictions** None (children welcome). **Terms** Deluxe (includes full breakfast). **Credit cards** All major cards.

Getting there N7/N8 to Mitchelstown, T38 to Mallow, N72 to Barraduff, R570 to Glenfesk church, N22 (Cork road), R (via Kilgarvin) to Kenmare (210 miles, 5 hrs). **Nearest airport** Shannon (110 miles). **Nearest rail station** Killarney. **Of local interest** Garinish Island; Bantry House (see p. 79). **Whole day expeditions** Ring of Kerry; Tours of Beara; Dingle Peninsula. **Refreshments/Dining out** Ballylickey Manor House (see p. 75); Blairs Cove, Durrus (dinners and Sunday lunch).

Quiet dignity

In 1714 Assolas House was owned by the Rev. Francis Gore. The main coaching road from Kanturk ran past the front door, and crossed the river beyond by a ford. The clergyman hung out a lantern each evening as dusk fell to guide travelers over the ford, and often rescued unfortunate wayfarers swept away when the river was in flood or when they were set-upon by highwaymen. He became well-loved locally for these charitable acts and the house became known in Gaelic as "Ata-Solas" – "Ford of Light." Perhaps the monks who once lived in a monastery on this site began the custom. Massive out-buildings, four-foot-deep walls, and a stone-flagged floor and wide hearth in the old kitchens remain from the 1600s. The house has two front doors. The original one faces the river, but in the early 18th century the gracious, lofty drawing room and dining room were added, linked by a wide stone-flagged hall to an elegant new Queen Anne front door facing towards what are now lawns, a grass tennis court, and seven acres of immaculate gardens and woodland walks on both sides of the river. There are a further 100 acres of fields and farmlands.

The house has been in the Bourke family for four generations. The present owner was running a business in Kanturk when he inherited Assolas. His wife and five children persuaded him, initially somewhat against his better judgement, to turn the house into a hotel. His wife studied at a catering college, modern kitchens were built, and all the children helped with the guests. All four daughters are now married, though one lives locally and returns in the evenings to help. The only son, Joe, is a trained cook and is now manager of Assolas. Guests are greeted by Mr and Mrs Bourke with quiet dignity, shown their pleasantly furnished bedrooms, and

served tea by the fire. Later, a table at the end of the drawing room, which is well-provided with comfortable chairs, is laid with an assortments of drinks, which the Bourkes serve to their dinner guests, who may then continue to replenish their own glasses, noting their choice on a pad provided. When I dined there on Sunday evening (to the accompaniment of taped religious music), I was served lobster wrapped in pasta, duck broth, poached salmon with hollandaise, almond and orange tart with thick cream, coffee, and petits fours. All were enjoyable. My room (with modern ensuite bathroom) was furnished with both a double and a single bed with white woven covers, a vast antique wardrobe, a cast-iron Victorian grate, and a fitted carpet.

This is a peaceful place, where you can sit and contemplate the swans gliding picturesquely on the river, and hear only the sound of the wind in the tall trees. The Rev. Francis Gore would be pleased to know that after so many years, travelers are still welcomed and well cared for at Assolas House.

A peaceful, timeless atmosphere surrounds Assolas: two corners of the gardens are shown opposite; above, a swan floats on the river that runs by the house.

ASSOLAS COUNTRY HOUSE HOTEL, Kanturk, Co. Cork. **Tel.** Kanturk (029) 50015. **Telex No. Fax** (029) 50795. **Owners** The Bourke family. **Manager** Joe Bourke. **Open** End March–early Nov. **Rooms** 10 double, all with bathroom (with wall shower), radio. **Facilities** Drawing room, dining room, old kitchens for private meals, meetings, small conferences; gardens, 100-acre farm, river, tennis (grass), boating, croquet, fishing. Helicopter landing. **Lunch** No. **Restrictions** No pets in house. **Terms** Expensive (includes full breakfast). Low season reductions. **Credit cards** All major cards. **Getting there** N8 to Mitchelstown, N73 to Mallow, N72, look for house signs after 9 miles (160 miles, 4 hrs). **Nearest airport** Shannon (55 miles). **Nearest rail station** Mallow. **Of local interest** Many castles (Mallow, Kanturk, Lismore); gardens at Ann's Grove, Doneraile, etc.; Blarney Castle. **Whole day expeditions** Killarney; Ring of Kerry; Cork. **Refreshments** Many small pubs (ask owner). **Dining out** Longueville House, Mallow (see p. 71).

Rural splendors

This impressive Georgian mansion stands in an imposing situation, looking down towards the Blackwater river through a fine group of oaks, planted in the battle formation of the French and English armies at Waterloo, and across to a prospect of distant mountains. The land upon which it stands was for centuries owned by the O'Callaghan clan, whose ruined Dromineen Castle on the cliffs above the Blackwater river can be seen from Longueville House. Taken from them in 1650 by Cromwell, the land eventually passed to the Longfield family; Richard Longfield was ennobled in 1795, taking the title Baron Longueville, hence the name of the house. By a satisfying twist of fortune, the land has come back into O'Callaghan hands at last, for the father of the present owner, the late Senator William O'Callaghan, bought it back in 1938.

Longueville House has an intriguing dual personality. Its exterior is magnificent: the central portion was built in 1720 and the wings and porch added at the end of the 18th century. Notable architectural features include a handsome hall door and fanlight, some fine ceilings, a carved white marble Adam fireplace, inlaid mahogany doors, and a splendid double staircase. The rooms are hung with portraits and ornate mirrors in heavy gilt frames. But at the same time the house is a family farmstead: there is a huge farmyard at the back with a range of farm buildings, passing tractors, kittens, children, dogs, and – somewhat surprisingly – a clipped maze. There is none of the stiff formality you might expect from the grand exterior – the welcome is friendly, and in the evening, when I came down to dinner, although some guests were sitting in the gracious drawing room, or watching television in the library, others had

been swept into the happy celebrations of a large cheerful informally dressed family party in the bar, for which a long festive table was prepared in the Presidents' Restaurant. An excellent dinner was served by friendly ladies in this striking room, which is hung with portraits of former Presidents of Ireland and opens onto a Victorian conservatory, designed by the celebrated Richard Turner.

Bedrooms have recently been refurbished in country-house style, and have tiled bathrooms; rooms at the top of the house are more simply furnished, and are less expensive. Telephones and televisions have been installed. My bedroom – which ran the length of the house – looked out both at the mountains and into the courtyard, so large it resembles a small village. The farm has its own vineyard (the only one in Ireland); although it does not bear fruit every year, it produces a dry white wine. Here is an unusual combination: the grandeur of a stately home and the friendliness of a working family farm.

The splendid staircase and handsome sitting room are memorable features of this architecturally distinguished hotel (opposite). Guests can enjoy wine produced by the hotel's own vineyard (above).

LONGUEVILLE HOUSE AND PRESIDENTS' RESTAURANT, Mallow, Co. Cork. **Tel.** Mallow (022) 47156. **Telex** 75498. **Fax** (022) 47459. **Owners** Michael and Jane O'Callaghan. **Open** 1 March–20 Dec. **Rooms** 13 double, 4 single, all with bathroom and hairdryer. (TV and direct-dial phones are being installed.) **Facilities** Drawing room, library, bar, restaurant, small conference facilities, own fishing on Blackwater river, 500-acre wooded estate, golf and riding nearby, by arrangement. Helicopter landing. **Lunch** Yes. **Restrictions** None. **Terms** Expensive. Reductions in low season. **Credit cards** All major cards. **Getting there** N8/N73 (149 miles, 3½ hrs). Hotel 3½ miles w of town on N72. 54 miles from Shannon. **Nearest airport** Cork. **Nearest rail station** Mallow. **Of local interest** Blarney Castle and grounds; Anne's Grove gardens; Doneraile Court and park; Spencer's Castle, Buttevant. **Whole day expeditions** Kinsale; Bantry (for Bantry House, see p. 79); Ring of Kerry; Adare; Kenmare; lakes. Dingle Peninsula. **Refreshments/Dining out** Many small pubs in Mallow with music (ask owners); Arbutus Lodge, Cork (see p. 85); Ahern's Seafood Bar, Youghal; Doyle's Seafood Bar, Dingle; Blue Haven, Kinsale; Ballylickey Manor, Bantry (see p. 75).

A warmly welcoming home

You have only to make one visit to Jeremy and Merrie Green to feel you have known them forever. They are so welcoming that it would be a pleasure to stay with them even if they did not live in such a fine Georgian mansion with excellent fishing. People who desire the impersonal ministrations of a hotel should go elsewhere; this is a family house, and Jeremy and Merrie do everything themselves, helped by friendly local ladies who have been with them for years.

Ballyvolane was Jeremy's childhood home. He laments the fact that the Victorians modernized the original 1728 house in 1847, adding single-pane windows and altering the pitch of the roof, but the gracious pillared hall, probably by the same architect who designed Cashel Palace (see page 49), the fine staircase, and the chandelier-hung dining room with its original shutters and big fireplace remained intact. The enormous stone-flagged Victorian kitchens are a challenge. When Jeremy and Merrie took over the house the large and gracious drawing room had somewhat eccentrically been turned into a huge family kitchen, with modern fittings one end, a group of settees round the elegant fireplace, and a big pine kitchen table near the door, overlooking the neatly trimmed terraced lawns and tall mature trees in the garden. The Greens hope one day to reinstate the original kitchens, and to return the drawing room to its former formal glory.

Guests dine in state, with silver candlesticks on the polished table in the grand dining room. Merrie is an expert cook who enjoys catching her own fish. Meat is from local farms, and most of the vegetables are produced by Jeremy's efforts in the enormous walled garden – I noted large asparagus beds. My dinner

included salmon caught that morning and home-grown raspberries. There is a sitting room for guests, once the study, with an open fire, though they tend to be drawn irresistibly to the kitchen, where they are plied with freshly-baked cakes – I found a French family who have returned each summer for several years sitting at the kitchen table contentedly shelling peas.

Merrie is currently refurbishing the bedrooms, making new bedcovers and curtains; when I stayed she was just putting the finishing touches to a front room, using a pine-green fabric starred with small white and yellow flowers, pretty against primrose walls. My bedroom looked out over the immaculate gardens. There was a duvet comforter on the bed, a huge wardrobe, the walls were pine-clad, and the bathroom had its original vast bath, enclosed in mahogany, with two steps to climb. Although the rooms are simple, they are large and comfortable, and well-supplied with books and magazines. Some guests just spend their entire visit fishing with Merrie; all are made to feel very welcome.

The back of the house (opposite, above) looks on to well-tended gardens; the pillared entrance hall (opposite, below) is a surviving Georgian interior in an interesting house modernized by the Victorians. A splendid mahogany bath appears above.

BALLYVOLANE HOUSE, Castlelyons, Co. Cork. **Tel.** Castlelyons (025) 36349. **Telex** 75800. **Fax** (058) 54744. **Owners** Jeremy and Merrie Green. **Open** All year. **Rooms** 5 double, 1 with bathroom ensuite, 2 with own bathroom adjacent, 2 sharing bathroom (1 bathroom has wall shower, 1 has hand shower). **Facilities** Drawing room, sitting room with TV and video, dining room, garden and grounds, croquet, table tennis, rough shooting, 8 miles fishing on Blackwater river, tennis, riding nearby. Helicopter landing. **Lunch** Picnics or snacks only. **Restrictions** None. **Terms** Moderate (includes full breakfast). **Credit cards** Access, Amex, Visa. **Getting there** N7 to Port Laoise, N8 through Fermoy, first L after speed limit, first R through Castlelyons and Bridesbridge and crossroads, then fork L, house 1 mile on R. (145 miles, 3½ hrs). 70 miles from Shannon. **Nearest airport** Cork. **Nearest rail station** Cork. **Of local interest** Gardens at Anne's Grove; Lismore Castle; Lakemount; Fota House (gardens and wildlife park); Riverstoun House; Cork. **Whole day expeditions** Kinsale; Blarney Castle; Ring of Kerry; Dingle Peninsula; Bunratty Castle; Waterford (crystal factory); Cashel. **Refreshments** Grand Hotel, Fermoy. **Dining out** Ballymaloe House, Shanagarry (see p. 87); Arbutus Lodge, Cork (see p. 85); Lovett's, Cork; Ahearne's Seafood Bar, Youghal.

Beside Bantry Bay

Bantry Bay is scattered with small islands, glimpsed between the hills as one travels past. On the day I arrived the landscape was drowsing in Mediterranean-like summer sunshine. I dropped into Ballylickey Manor House for an exploratory cup of tea, and found it served in the pool-side restaurant; it was accompanied by a large slice of fruit cake, warm scones, and home-made shortbread. Eyeing the heated pool wistfully, I asked to be shown over the hotel, and, discovering that the spacious bedroom called Narcissus was free that night, instantly revised my schedule and booked in. This room was in the house; there are also pool-side cottages, prettily furnished and tempting.

Built about 1650 by Lord Kenmare as a shooting lodge, Ballylickey has been owned for four generations by the Franco-Irish Graves family (relatives of poet Robert Graves). In 1946 it was converted into a hotel, which was totally refurbished in 1982. There is a small downstairs sitting room and a dining room used in winter, delightfully furnished with excellent antiques and a most attractive blend of old prints and oils, painted fans, and vivid modern patchwork pictures in silk. There are fitted carpets throughout. The eaves bedrooms are spacious and equally intriguingly furnished. Mine had a vast bed, with a white cover inset with small bands of bright ribbons, echoed in a wall hanging and cushions. Dressing table and creamy sheets were trimmed with broderie, cream curtains had a pattern of big blue flowers, matching the plain blue bedhead and easy chairs. There was a big walk-in closet, and the furniture included a walnut tallboy, an antique lyre-shaped cheval glass, and a small painted and gilded antique table. Early hand-colored bird-prints, fresh flowers, and a wide window seat on which to curl up and enjoy the view to the Bay completed an attractive ensemble. The dark-green-tiled bathroom had finely striped red and green paper, pine shelves, an excellent shower, and plenty of big soft towels.

Dinner was a delight. A sherry beside the pool was followed by smoked salmon, orange and apricot soup, lamb with rosemary grilled on an open wood fire, salad, and fresh strawberries. The restaurant is furnished and decorated with the same individual flair and charm as the house. As the evening cooled, the sliding doors were closed, and the poolside gardens floodlit. Next morning the covers were taken off the heated pool for me to take a dip before breakfast, which was served on flowery Portmeiron china and big dark-blue hand-glazed plates, with coffee in a handsome silver pot.

Sun, peace, unspoilt sea views, the understated simple excellence of the French-style cooking, and the stylishness of the decor reminded me of the French Riviera before the concrete tide of buildings changed it for ever.

Ballylickey is set in beautiful surroundings amid terraced gardens looking onto Bantry Bay (opposite and overleaf). The expert French cuisine (above) is most memorable.

BALLYLICKEY MANOR HOUSE, Ballylickey, Bantry Bay, Co. Cork. **Tel.** Bantry (027) 50071. **Telex** 75837. **Fax No.** **Owners** Mr and Mrs C.W.G. Graves. **Open** April–1 Nov. **Rooms** 6 double, 5 suites, all with bathroom (with wall shower), TV, phone (not direct). **Facilities** Sitting room, dining room in house, restaurant/bar/sitting room by pool, heated pool, gardens, water gardens, croquet lawn, own river and sea fishing. Helicopter landing. **Lunch** Yes. **Terms** Expensive. **Restrictions** Dogs by arrangement only. **Credit cards** Amex, Visa. **Getting there** N7/N8, N22, R585. Hotel on coast road at Ballylickey. (220 miles, 5½ hrs.) 120 miles from Shannon. **Nearest airport** Cork. **Nearest rail station** Cork. **Of local interest** Bantry House (see p. 79); Garinish Island; Glengarriff Garden; Dursey Island. **Whole day expeditions** Ring of Beara; Ring of Kerry; Muckross House and gardens; Killarney and lakes; coastal road to Schull, Baltimore, Skibbereen, etc. **Refreshments/Dining out** Blairs Cove Restaurant, Durrus (nr Bantry); Park Hotel, Kenmare (see p. 67); snacks at Bantry House, Bantry (see p. 79); Shiro (Japanese restaurant), Ahakista.

Maintaining Ireland's heritage

The large stone gateway leading to Bantry House is in the middle of the village, opposite the quay and the colorful fishing boats. From here a long drive climbs up, edged with rhododendrons, emerging at last to a fine pair of black and gold wrought-iron gates, and a wide gravel forecourt. In the middle is a huge circular flowerbed, in which a clipped hedge rings a statue of Diana the huntress; more statuary and great urns spilling over with bright flowers stand on the wide terraces overlooking the bay. Bantry House, begun in about 1700, was bought by Richard White in 1750. His grandson helped to organize local resistance to a French invasion in 1796, and was made a Baron, and later an Earl, by a grateful George III. His restless great-grandson toured Europe, gathering a fine art collection, brought back to Bantry House, which was enlarged to house it. Added to since then, it now includes 15th- and 16th-century Russian icons, the rose-pink Aubusson tapestries made for Marie Antoinette on her marriage to the Dauphin, Louis XV's Gobelin tapestries which once hung in Versailles, and fine Sheraton, Irish Hepplewhite, and inlaid Boulle furniture.

Egerton Shelswell-White, a keen classical and jazz trombone player, was farming in Alabama when he inherited Bantry House. He has recently converted a self-contained wing into six comfortable bedrooms, with fitted carpets and ensuite modern bathrooms. He has installed new, good-quality beds with duvet-comforters, pretty fabrics, armchairs, some antique furniture, and central heating. My room, on the top floor, rewarded me for a steepish climb with a marvellous view over the bay. Others look out over the gardens, and there are further simpler and more economical family rooms. There is a breakfast room downstairs and a tiny sitting area. The delightful kitchens at the back of the house, with black-leaded range, big cauldrons, pine tables and benches, and a craftshop, are open for snacks during the day. Egerton's charming Austrian wife will prepare a light dinner – grilled trout or chops, for instance, with salad and fruit – if warned well in advance, and if commitments to their small children allow. Groups of more than ten (again only by prior arrangement) may dine in immense splendor in the ornate and lofty dining room of the main house.

Visitors come from all over the world to visit Bantry House. The rooms are for the independent who want to enjoy the gardens at leisure, and tour the area. A key is provided (to the wing, not to the main house), the Whites and their staff are friendly and helpful, but stress that rather than running expensive "house-parties," they are putting their maximum effort into maintaining, restoring, and keeping open for future generations this splendid piece of Ireland's heritage.

Bantry House is seen here (opposite) from the top of its terraced gardens, looking towards Bantry Bay. A corner of the gardens appears above; overleaf are (left) one of the tapestries made for Marie Antoinette and (right) views of the dining room and stables.

BANTRY HOUSE, Bantry, Co. Cork. **Tel.** Bantry (027) 50047. **Telex** No. **Fax** No. **Owners** Mr and Mrs E. Shelswell-White. **Open** All year (except Christmas Day). **Rooms** 10 double, 6 with ensuite bathrooms, all with direct-dial phone and TV. **Facilities** Small sitting area, breakfast room, restaurant/café, sea fishing and riding, by arrangement. Small conference facilities. **Lunch** Snacks served in restaurant. **Terms** Moderate (includes full breakfast). An extra fee is charged to view the house. **Restrictions** No pets in rooms. **Credit cards** Access, Amex, Visa. **Getting there** N7/N8 to Cork, N22, L on R584 (218 miles, 5½ hrs). 120 miles from Shannon. **Nearest airport** Cork. **Nearest rail station** Cork. **Of local interest** Tour of Bantry House; Garinish Island (gardens); Glengarriff Gardens; Dursey Islands. **Whole day expeditions** Ring of Beara; Ring of Kerry; Muckross House and gardens and Killarney and lakes; coastal road to Schull, Baltimore, etc.; Kinsale. **Refreshments/Dining out** Ballylickey Manor House (see p. 75); Blair's Cove Restaurant, Durrus (nr Bantry); Park Hotel Kenmare (see p. 67); Great Southern Hotel, Killarney (see p. 63).

26 Scilly House

Civilized simplicity

Kinsale is a charming little yachting harbor with an international population. It has a huge bay, at the mouth of which are two impressive 17th-century forts. There are houses dotted about on the steep slopes, including gray-tile-hung 18th-century Scilly House (named perhaps by fishermen who settled here from the Scilly Isles). Behind a high wall with wrought-iron gates is a small gravelled front courtyard, while at the back, mature, secluded gardens drop away sharply to the harbor and a cluster of brightly-painted small cottages. Trees frame the magnificent views over the bay. My bedroom, with white-painted iron bedstead, duvet-comforter, pretty chintz, and a bathroom with a huge apricot-colored bath, had a sitting room with rattan furniture and a panoramic view. I sat entranced and watched the yachts sail home, the sun set, and next morning the water turn palest blue and silver at dawn.

Karin Young, a watercolor artist from California, fell in love with village, view, and house. With Bill Skelly, erstwhile band-leader and singer from Belfast – who can still sometimes be persuaded to sing hauntingly sweet and sad Irish songs at the house baby grand – she has spent a year winning back a wilderness garden and refurbishing the house. Since both have finished raising their families, they embarked on providing bed, breakfast, and (when requested) dinner for Kinsale's visitors. To the horror of purists, the house is furnished not with Georgian antiques, but with Karin's own possessions – antique American quilts on the walls, pine furniture, plenty of paintings and books, and decorative objects discovered on her travels. There are flowers from the garden, and big comfortable settees in front of the tiled Victorian hearths in both large sitting rooms. (They discovered tiles for the two-way hearth in the dining room when digging the garden, and have re-assembled them like a jigsaw puzzle.)

Scilly House, it is believed, was once owned by the commander of the fort who, finding his daughter's soldier sweetheart asleep on duty, shot him, causing her to fling herself from the ramparts, which she is now said to haunt, a sad figure dressed in white. In 1601 Kinsale was briefly occupied by the Spanish fleet, who joined up with the Irish for a land battle, but were defeated by the British. Alexander Selkirk set out in 1703 from Kinsale, to be shipwrecked, and provide the inspiration for Defoe's *Robinson Crusoe*. There is a friendly community of fishermen, yachtsmen, innkeepers, writers, and artists who all know each other, and enjoy convivial evenings in the many little pubs and restaurants which serve outstanding fresh fish and shellfish, and – like Karin and Bill – make visitors to this idyllic place warmly welcome.

The interiors of Scilly House are delightfully simple: opposite are one of the two sitting rooms (above) and a bedroom. The model ship above is an appropriate ornament for a house with a nautical setting.

SCILLY HOUSE, Kinsale, Co. Cork. **Tel.** Cork (021) 772413. **Telex** No. **Fax** No. **Owners** Karin Young and Bill Skelly. **Open** 1 March–Dec. **Rooms** 4 double, 2 suites, all with bathroom (incl. hand shower). **Facilities** Sitting room, library, dining room, garden, own boat. Fishing, shooting, riding, golf, by arrangement. **Lunch** Picnic lunch if requested. **Restrictions** No small children, no pets. **Terms** Moderate (includes full breakfast). **Credit cards** No. **Getting there** N7/N8, R600 (178 miles, 5 hrs). 90 miles from Shannon. **Nearest airport** Cork. **Nearest rail station** Cork. **Of local interest** In Kinsale: 12th-century church, 18th-century courthouse/museum; coastal villages. **Whole day expeditions** Bantry; Schull; Youghal; Fota Island. **Refreshments** Man Friday, Blue Haven, The Bistro, The Vintage, Max's Wine Bar, all in Kinsale. **Dining out** Ballymaloe House, Shanagarry (see p. 87); Arbutus Lodge, Cork (see p. 85).

Memorable cuisine

I must confess to a great partiality for the County of Cork. All round the coast of Ireland there are enchanting little fishing villages, but Cork seems particularly well provided with pleasant places to stay and eat, as well as picturesque drives both by the sea and inland and a great feeling of getting away from it all. There are excellent little fish restaurants, where everything on the menu is the catch of the day; at Arbutus Lodge your prospective dinner is plodding steadily round the lobster tank in the bar, feelers waving, claws clamped safely shut with broad elastic bands.

Arbutus Lodge is a notable eating place, run by the Ryan family, whose son Michael has trained in several of France's great kitchens. His Michelin-starred food is definitely worth a detour to sample. The house is on a steep hillside in Cork's fashionable Montenotte district; its prize-winning gardens contain camellias, rhododendrons, weeping silver limes, and of course an arbutus tree. By day there is a view of Cork's not-overly picturesque docks, transformed at night into a panoply of twinkling lights. Dating from the late 1700s, the house was built by a wealthy miller, sold to a master cooper made prosperous by the trade in casks of butter exported from Cork, and was in 1871 owned by Cork's Lord Mayor. Sir Daniel O'Sullivan, grandfather of film star Maureen O'Sullivan and great-grandfather of Mia Farrow, lived here for a while, and now the Ryans have turned it into a charming hotel.

From the ample parking space you enter the dark brown hall, where woodwork and plasterwork are picked out in white. A large comfortable bar hung with the work of contemporary Irish artists is on your right, and the lofty dining room straight ahead. Stairs go up past tall windows inset with colored glass

flowers to a broad landing. The Ryans are refurbishing their bedrooms "with whatever money the government leaves us," one at a time. Ask for their best room, with antique furniture, draped bed, and lavish marble bathroom with robes and Jean Patou toiletries, or one of the three more modern smaller rooms, also with splendid bathrooms. They have further rooms, more modestly priced, practical for a rapid visit but with conventional hotel furnishing. Sentimentally, hypocritically – since I so enjoy lobster – I avoided condemning one of the patient captives in the tank. Dinner was memorable for a warm salad of lamb's liver flavored with a hint of ginger, followed by nettle soup and breast of duck with garden peas, spinach, and the exceptional Irish potatoes. A trolley was well-laden with appetizing desserts, though I faint-heartedly dodged the chocolate cake and picked strawberry sorbet with a scattering of raspberries. The wine list has won prizes. This is somewhere to stay in comfort, eat meals to remember, and explore County Cork.

The porch (opposite, above right) leads to the charming hallway (opposite, below), beyond which stairs rise past tall windows with stained-glass flowers. The master bedroom is shown above.

ARBUTUS LODGE HOTEL, Montenotte, Cork, Co. Cork. **Tel.** Cork (021) 501237. **Telex** 75079. **Fax** (021) 502893. **Owners** The Ryan family. **Open** All year. **Rooms** 7 double, 9 single, 1 master, 3 superior, all with bathroom (4 with hand shower, 8 with wall shower), TV, direct-dial phone, minibar, radio, hair dryer, trouser press. 4 main rooms also with safe. **Facilities** Sitting room, dining room, bar, small conference facilities, gardens, parking. Rough shooting, riding, special all-inclusive fox-hunting holidays, by arrangement. **Lunch** Yes. **Restrictions** No pets. No cigars or pipes in dining room. **Terms** Expensive (includes full breakfast). **Credit cards** All major cards. **Getting there** See directions to Scilly House (160 miles, 4 hrs). 70 miles from Shannon. **Nearest airport** Cork. **Nearest rail station** Cork. **Of local interest** Fota House and gardens; Anne's Grove Gardens, Castletown Roche; Riverstone House; Muckross House and gardens. **Whole day expeditions** Blarney Castle; Killarney; Bantry House. **Refreshments** Ask owners about local pubs; pubs and small restaurants in Kinsale (see p. 83). **Dining out** Ballymaloe House, Shanagarry (see p. 87); Ahearne's Seafood Bar, Youghal.

Hospitable home of a famous chef

Ivan and Myrtle Allen moved to Ballymaloe just after World War II. Its farm provided marvellous fresh eggs, butter, meat, vegetables, and fruit, while sea and river close by yielded a great variety of fish and shellfish. As their children grew, and Myrtle became an ever-more-expert cook, she decided in 1964 to open The Yeats Room restaurant, hung with pictures by the poet's artist brother, Jack. Three years later she opened a few bedrooms. Helped by her children, advised on wines by her husband, Myrtle Allen swiftly became the doyenne of Irish cooks, and has added a cookery school, wine and craft shops, and more bedrooms.

Do not come expecting some designer-decorated executive retreat. This is still a family farmhouse, a lovely rambling Georgian building, with big sash windows, and on one corner the remaining 15th-century tower of the castle that belonged to the Fitzgeralds for nearly two hundred years. They were dispossessed by Cromwell, who visited the castle, as did William Penn. Some say the building is haunted by the dwarf Chuff, who, together with a jester, once lived here. Their portraits, painted in the 1700s, were returned to hang here in the drawing room in 1967.

Ballymaloe stands amid fields of grazing sheep. Visitors park in a courtyard with big trees, outside the craft shop full of tempting hand-made pottery, knitware, silver, and books, and walk in over the paved stone forecourt. People may be playing croquet on the front lawn, while children splash in the heated pool, and toddlers grub with total concentration in a large sandpit. Sand is tracked into the house: nobody bothers, as it is polished away every evening. The hall is wide and light-filled, hung with elk-horns dug up on the farm, and pleasing modern pictures. Hand-woven rugs are on the floor. Bedrooms are simple; mine had an antique bed, pale green walls, white woven bedcover, a bunch of daisies in a vase, and a tiny bathroom with shower tucked in. There are also new bedrooms with big modern bathrooms.

My dismay at hearing there was only a buffet meal on a Sunday vanished when I saw the table of food. It was piled high with pâtés, oysters, crab, lobster, mussels, a whole salmon, prawns, a cucumber and yoghurt ring, courgette-flower and five other salads, tiny tomatoes just picked, and huge roasts: turkey, pressed spiced beef, rib roast, a goose, a vast ham, pork with crackling. Anyone able to face the thought was invited to sample creamy desserts and great bowls of freshly picked raspberries and strawberries, and home-made icecreams. Ballymaloe has a wonderfully tranquil and happy atmosphere, and the best home-raised, home-cooked food in Ireland.

The view from Ballymaloe across fields appears opposite; a selection of Myrtle Allen's home-baked bread is shown above. Overleaf (left) are a corner of the courtyard and a table laid with breakfast; on the right is the hotel's front door.

BALLYMALOE HOUSE, Shanagarry, Midleton, Co. Cork. **Tel.** Midleton (021) 652531. **Telex** 75208. **Fax** (021) 652021. **Owners** Ivan and Myrtle Allen. **Open** All year, except 24–26 December. **Rooms** 28 double, 2 single, all with bathroom (26 with wall shower), direct-dial phone. **Facilities** Drawing room, dining room (four interconnected rooms), heated pool (closed in winter), tennis, croquet, gardens and grounds, river and pond, helicopter landing, riding and fishing by arrangement, conferences in winter. **Lunch** Yes. **Restrictions** No pets in rooms. **Terms** Expensive (reductions in winter). **Credit cards** All major cards. **Getting there** N7 to Port Laoise, N8 through Fermoy to Rathcormac, R on R626 to Midleton, R629 to Shanagarry. 90 miles from Shannon. **Nearest airport** Cork. **Nearest rail station** Cork. **Of local interest** Countryside and beaches; Fota Island; Youghal; Riverstown House. **Whole day expeditions** Kinsale; Bantry; Cashel. **Refreshments** Little local pubs (ask owners). **Dining out** Arbutus Lodge, Cork (see p. 85).

Irish romance

Lady Levinge of Clohamon (see page 47) was born in this castle, which stands on its own 310-acre island in the middle of the river Suir. She remembers Christmases in front of the enormous fireplace in the Great Hall with the Fitzgerald coat of arms carved on the massive stone chimney-breast, Elizabethan oak panelling, huge beams, and ornate plasterwork ceiling. There was the excitement of waiting on the river bank to watch her brother, home for the holidays from boarding school, being rowed across the river. Her grandfather, much married, was a noted local personality, her mother, who later became Princess d'Ardia Caracciolo, was a famous thirties beauty, who, it is said, had been known to swim the river when returning home from a hunt ball. The castle was built in the 1160s and had wings added in the 19th century. Now it has been bought by a wealthy local farmer and transformed into a comfortable and luxurious hotel.

A small private ferry takes visitors and their vehicles over the 300 yards of river, where a large elegant launch is tied up waiting to take guests deep-sea fishing. The drive, edged with lamps, curves round through the woods, to immaculate gardens, lawns, and a tarmac forecourt in front of the massive stone towers of the crenelated castle. The big arched entrance leads straight into the Great Hall, with a reception desk in one bay. At one end of the Hall is the vast panelled dining room, with another ornate ceiling, from which leads a light-filled conservatory furnished in rattan, a small breakfast room, and a comfortable drawing room. An oak staircase rises to what were once the master bedrooms, now suites, great lofty rooms, some with antique four-posters and bathrooms still with original tile-work. All have striking reproduction claw-footed baths and bathroom-ware painted with flowers, with brass taps and wooden seats.

At the other end of the Hall are smaller, more snug bedrooms. Mine had pale green wallpaper with a swagged frieze, mullioned stone windows, and a pretty white quilted bedcover. There was a pair of tall green and white Chinese bedside lamps, a Victorian fireplace tiled in dark green, a desk, and – since it was a corner room – views over the river in two directions. It was centrally heated, and had an enormous bathroom and big clothes closet. Everywhere was close-carpeted. A beautifully arranged plate of fresh fruit and chocolates on a starched napkin, a bottle of local spring water, a selection of magazines, and a large remote-control television completed my creature comforts; tea when requested was swiftly brought to the room. There are fresh flowers everywhere. I enjoyed my dinner: a warm duck salad, fresh tomato soup, local salmon, vegetables grown on the island, and apple tart with cream, all of the highest quality, and pleasantly and formally served. This is a most romantically situated hotel.

The Fitzgerald coat of arms is proudly displayed over the huge fireplace in the entrance hall (opposite). The bathroom above retains its original tiles. Overleaf is a view of the castle from its gardens; the river is visible through the trees.

WATERFORD CASTLE, The Island, Ballinakill, Waterford, Co. Waterford. **Tel.** Waterford (051) 78203. **Telex** 80332. **Fax** (051) 79316. **Owner** Edward J. Kearns, Waterford Castle Ltd. **Manager** Richard Sherwood. **Open** All year. **Rooms** 12 double, 5 suites, all with bathroom (with hand and wall showers), TV, direct-dial phone, radio, room service. **Facilities** Drawing room/Hall, sitting room, breakfast room, restaurant, elevator, heated indoor pool, gardens, croquet, snooker, 310-acre estate, own river and deep-sea fishing, shooting, riding, hunting, and polo. Helicopter landing, ferry, launch, courtesy car (Jaguar XJ6). **Lunch** Yes. **Restrictions** No pets. **Terms** Deluxe. **Credit cards** All major cards. **Getting there** N9/N10 (98 miles, 3 hrs). 78 miles from Shannon. **Nearest airport** Cork. **Nearest rail station** Waterford. **Of local interest** Waterford crystal factory; Mount Congreve Estate; Dunmore East, Passage East, Ballyhack villages. **Whole day expeditions** Kennedy Park; Wexford via ferry; fishing trips, golf outings; shooting and fox hunting in season. **Refreshments** Small restaurants in Waterford (ask hotel). **Dining out** Nothing nearby.

Friendly charm

A castle stood on this land in the 1400s, and beyond a high wall in the garden is an ancient stableyard with Elizabethan buildings, said to be haunted by the ghost of a former owner, who was piked to death by insurrectionists in 1798. The French family, previous owners of Newbay House, founded the Canadian Mounties. The last heir married a Canadian girl, and settled in Canada, selling Newbay House to Paul and Min Drum. Paul is charming, energetic, and an excellent trained cook, with an imposing moustache; his slightly Spanish looks were inherited from his mother, a noted singer. He and his delightful slim blonde wife Min, Irish of Dutch extraction, once owned a larger fashionable Dublin hotel (chic Dublin gourmet restaurant Le Coq Hardi is run by their former chef), but having now three rapidly-growing children, they prefer to be in this quiet rural retreat. The house was sadly run-down, but fascinated them by its mixture of classical Georgian symmetry and odd bits built on by the Victorians, including a vast wing as big as the original house. The bow-ended drawing room and elegant dining room have kept their long sash windows and original shutters, and Paul and Min decided to leave intact the additions, which added character to the house, and content themselves with restoring Newbay House to a comfortable home.

Open peat and log fires welcome arriving guests, and the house is decorated with stripped pine furniture which Paul restores and sells, notably to Macy's of New York. Min makes the patchwork covers for the four-poster pine beds (made by Paul), which have duvet comforters. Paul's collection of top-hats, solar topees, and plumed helmets is on the top of a carved antique Austrian tall-boy in the drawing room; a still-working symphonion stands in the hall; marble-topped washstands are in the bathrooms (which also have modern showers). There are huge trees, lawns, and bright flowerbeds in the garden, from which Min picks flowers to decorate the house, and gathers plants to dry for pretty arrangements. There is a pond with wild ducks and moorhens, a peacock which strolls grandly about and poses on the porch above the kitchen door, a black-and-white cat rescued when dumped as a tiny kitten in their dustbin, and a slightly odd-looking dog, Murdoch, a labrador-basset-hound-cross-by-mistake, all friendly but not intrusive; housemartins nest under the eaves.

This is not a hotel: you must book in advance, and you will not find hotel facilities. It is like staying with friends. Paul's cooking, tasty, with generous servings, is much better and more varied than that of most hotels (Min is also an excellent cook) and you will have been very well cared for. Newbay House is a delight to visit.

The sitting room and dining room are comfortable and welcoming (opposite). The pond in the garden (above) is home for a variety of wildfowl.

NEWBAY COUNTRY HOUSE, Newbay, Wexford, Co. Wexford. **Tel.** Wexford (053) 22779. **Telex** No. **Fax** No. **Owners** Paul and Min Drum. **Open** 17 March–31 Oct. (at other times occasional private parties by arrangement). **Rooms** 5 double, 2 with ensuite bathroom (with shower), all with 4-poster beds. **Facilities** Drawing room, dining room, gardens and grounds, helicopter landing. **Restrictions** No pets. **Terms** Moderate (includes full breakfast). **Credit cards** No. **Getting there** N11 (88 miles, 2½ hrs). 150 miles from Shannon. **Nearest airport** Dublin. **Nearest rail station** Wexford. **Of local interest** Wexford opera festival in October; Wexford (quay with fishing boats, town); Johnstown Castle and park; wildfowl reserve; Tacumshane Windmill; Kilmore village and quay; John F. Kennedy Park; Our Lady's Island (pilgrimage place). **Whole day expeditions** Saltee Islands Bird Sanctuary; Russborough House and art collection; via ferry to Waterford (crystal factories); Courtown beaches; Dublin. **Refreshments** Oak Tavern, Kelly's, The Bohemian Girl, The Lobster Pot, The Granary, all in Wexford. **Dining out** Marlfield House, Gorey (see p. 43); Clohamon House, Bunclody (see p. 47), by arrangement only.

Index